IN THE
FOOTSTEPS
OF THE
BUDDHA

IN THE FOOTSTEPS OF THE BUDDHA

by Marc de Smedt

FRANCES LINCOLN

In the Footsteps of the Buddha
English language translation by Ian West © Frances Lincoln Limited 2000
Original French text © Éditions Albin Michel S.A. – Paris 1991

Text first published in France in 1981 by Éditions Retz

Published in 1991 by Éditions Albin Michel S.A., 22, rue Huyghens, 75014 Paris

British Library Cataloguing in Publication Data available on request

ISBN 0-7112-1586-3

Set in Angie

Printed in Hong Kong

1 3 5 7 9 8 6 4 2

To a great Zen Master no longer with us:
Taisen Deshimaru

– M. de S.

CONTENTS

Modern place-names are followed by ancient names in italics.

MAP OF THE BUDDHA'S ROUTE,
WITH PRINCIPAL PLACES OF INTEREST

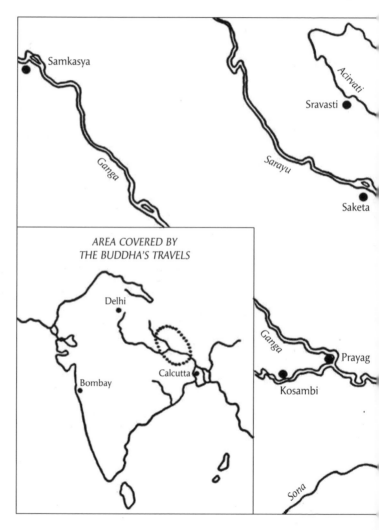

Map uses ancient forms of place-names.

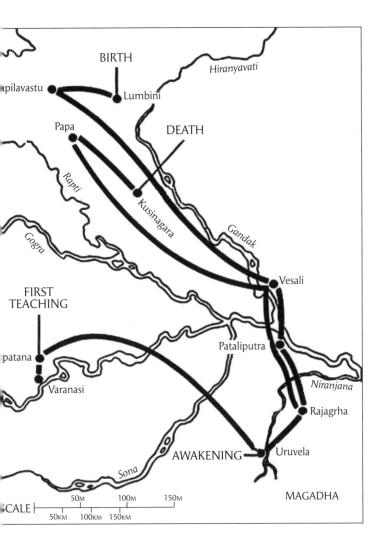

BIRTH

Hiranyavati

Kapilavastu

Lumbini

Papa

DEATH

Rapti

Kusinagara

Gandak

Gogra

Vesali

FIRST
TEACHING

Pataliputra

patana

Niranjana

Varanasi

Rajagrha

AWAKENING

Uruvela

Sona

MAGADHA

50M   100M   150M

SCALE

50KM   100KM 150KM

INTRODUCTION

This literary ramble in the footsteps of the Buddha owes its origins to three aspects of my own experience. Firstly, for years I had been fascinated by the personality, life and message of this sage whose world was that of India 2,500 years ago, but whose enigmatic smile still haunts our dreams of attaining fulfilment, exploring wider horizons and expanding the limits of consciousness. Then there was my almost daily practice of *zazen* (seated meditation) which forms the basis of Zen. Finally, in the autumn of 1980, I undertook a journey which led me in search of the background to the Buddha's long life, to the north of India – the present-day provinces of Bihar and Uttar Pradesh –

and to Nepal: a 1,875 mile (3,000 km) symbolic pilgrimage to the source. Symbolic, for we are certainly in a very different age if a lifetime of eighty years or so – of which some fifty were spent not only on the move, but also on foot – can be retraced in a matter of weeks. All of which is beside the point, for this was a journey I felt I had to make. These harmless fancies should be indulged; dreams unfulfilled are liable to turn sour. And, in the beauty of the country and the wealth of new cultural experiences, the rewards were overwhelming ...

The resulting book is a patchwork of notes, purely personal reactions and recollections, jotted down during each evening's halt in my wanderings: snatches of discussions with the Buddha's disciples, memorable words and parables. These are mere threads from a rich and complex tapestry of dialogues, selected by way of example, together with a few overall reflections on my adventure. Yet how inadequate I find my observations in comparison with the discoveries of this Enlightener. His practices and revelations gave birth to a religion and philosophy which, in these unhappy times, remains as inspirational and relevant as ever to the way we live our lives. I am not suggesting that we should all become Buddhists; merely that, in the words of Dogen (a thirteenth-century Zen monk), 'every being contains the Buddha-nature'. It is up to us to discover it.

Four key encounters decided the destiny of Prince Gautama, who was to become the Buddha, the Enlightened or Awakened One. These confrontations (the Four Signs) revolutionized the outlook of a man who appeared to enjoy all the blessings that life could offer. He was surrounded, according to legend, by nothing but pleasure, women and the colourful sights and sounds of the court. He was the father of a fine son, and heir to a respected kingdom. Yet he was to experience spiritual devastation when he stumbled upon an old man decrepit with age, a sick man being tended by friends and family, death in the form of a corpse wrapped in its shroud, and the detached wisdom of a wandering *sadhu*. The latter – half-saint, half-madman – holding appearances in contempt, had divined that the true foundations of reality lay elsewhere.

These encounters sufficed to impress upon the prince – young and hitherto protected from every imperfection of the outside world – that all was impermanence, suffering and vanity, and that the true sense of life was unknown. This crisis led him to abandon his palace, his kingdom and his family to wander the earth in search of the true meaning

13

of life and an understanding of human destiny. For what reply was there to the eternal question: what is the purpose of existence?

The answers which he discovered in the course of his quest, the example he set, his teaching and his practices set in motion one of the most powerful religious currents in history. Buddhism, for example, is the only creed never to have sparked off a war.

Returning to the Buddha's character, I would only say that beneath all his fame and success as a sage, there lies a human being to whom our hearts reach out. The *sutras* summarizing his teaching were not formally arranged till after his death, and contain notable embellishments and excesses of style. The legends of his life are also full of exaggeration. Yet through these many layers one ceaselessly catches the bright gleam of a personality whose mind and actions were attuned to the needs of others, and who was full of warmth towards his fellow men and all creation. Here was a man who decided to journey to the limits of himself on a remorseless quest which would lead him, in the starkness of his honesty, to the very frontiers of death. Yet the day arrived when, in the wealth of such profoundly acquired experiences, he reached Enlightenment. The Truth behind the universe broke upon him like a tidal wave, and the age-old enigma was resolved. But he was not content to rest there, an austere figure enthroned on an Olympian cloud of self-satisfaction, like the popular Christian image of God the Father. On the contrary, this young man was to continue his journey. To the very end, he went on teaching and living life to the full, attempting to share with others – with anyone who was interested – what, in all humility, he called his 'discovery':

'Monks, I am as a man wandering through the jungle, through the great forest, who, all of a sudden, comes upon an ancient track, an old pathway trodden by generations past. And, following this pathway, the man arrives at an ancient town, a royal city once the home of men, with its parks, its pools and its walls: a place of great wonders. And he, retracing his steps, hurries to inform the king or his minister, saying, "There lies nearby a wonderful, ancient city, with a path leading to it. We must go without delay and live in this marvellous place, where men of old dwelt. Sire, you must build this city anew." And, following his counsel, the king and his ministers decide to rebuild the city, which once again becomes rich, well-populated and prosperous.

'I too, monks, have discovered an ancient pathway, an old road, once travelled by all enlightened and awakened persons of the past. Monks, what is this ancient way? It is the Eightfold Path, that is: perfect view, perfect resolve, perfect speech, perfect conduct, perfect livelihood, perfect effort, perfect mindfulness, perfect concentration. And by following this road, I have arrived at a place within me where I have come to understand the origin of life and death, the origin of suffering and of cessation ... I have arrived at a place where I have understood the meaning of voluntary desire, where I have understood the meaning of cessation; a place where the meaning of all that we do has been revealed.

'These things I learnt through my own experience. Afterwards, I began to lead along this path every man and woman who wished to follow it. My hope is that they will discover this place within themselves, that this place will once again emerge from obscurity and prosper; that it will become known to the greatest possible number, and be in the ears of all men, everywhere.'

Some twenty-five centuries ago, the Buddha discovered a path – a path open to all who, irrespective of caste, race, age, religion or belief, lay aside all prejudice and arbitrary distinctions and seek to understand the true nature of their existence.

BIRTH

Rummindai~*Lumbini*

It was here then, more than 2,500 years ago, that he was born, under a great *sal* tree like the one overhanging the pool. Its roots are amazing; people sit among them, using them like armchairs.

A few hours after leaving Gorakhpur in the soft light of dawn, and crossing the frontier which disappears somewhere in the middle of a village, we finally arrive in southern Nepal. You leave the proper road and plough on a few miles along a rugged track, all sand and stones, till you reach Rummindai – the old Lumbini – a handful of tumbledown wood-and-thatch buildings. We have come from India, but we could equally well have made the trip from Kathmandu by plane or bus. There is yet another route, a 280 mile (450 km) journey which takes at least two days via Pokhara and Bhairava through breathtaking scenery. The Indians and the Nepalese compete for the tourist trade, each side promoting its own 'special' tour of the pilgrim sites to groups of Buddhists from Japan, Sri Lanka and elsewhere. The planners are working on a vast tourist scheme, and all the wild, lonely places we went through are already earmarked for hotel development. The Buddha, it seems, is back in fashion.

We rest in the village, eating at a kind of booth. The table is filthy, but the plateful of curried lentils – washed down with scalding hot tea – tastes good. It is hot now; flies are buzzing round us, children run about playing in the dust, and the Nepalese stare at us with their warm and friendly smiles. To reach the place where the Buddha was born, we need to push on a few hundred yards through the village.

The vast *sal* tree is astonishing; it stands out on the plain in all its glory against the backdrop of the Himalayas. There are a few small temples in nearby clumps of trees, and I recognize some Tibetan prayer pennants. The desert-like landscape surrounding us – a kind of savannah – must once have been a jungle, and the Terai Forest, still harbouring tigers and elephants, is not far off. The place has an aura of joy; its vibrations are perfect, and there is the profoundest sensation of peace. Sitting among the roots of the tree, my gaze is lost for a while in the blueness of the sky and the water of the pool where the boy-king was bathed: the boy who was to become both pilgrim and Enlightener. I turn to watch the handful of people wandering round the ruins of Asoka's column. Asoka was a Buddhist emperor of the third century BCE who erected similar monuments at memorable places on the Buddha's itinerary. Nearby is a temple reached by a few steps. It has a tiny sanctuary where you can see Queen Maya Devi sculpted in the stonework. She is grasping a branch of the *sal* tree, and beside her is the newborn baby, Buddha, already seated on a lotus. From a cloud, two celestial figures shower him with flowers. There are other powerful statues on the site; some are mutilated, their faces smashed by the invading Muslims centuries ago.

Queen Maya brought her child into the world some distance from her palace – she was returning from her parents' house, where, according to tradition, she was expected to give birth. The joy of King Suddhodana

Gautama was immense: legend tells us that the royal couple had yearned for a child for twenty years. But his happiness was cruelly blighted. A few days later, the queen died, never having risen from her childbed. The boy was to be brought up by her sister, who named him Siddhartha ('accomplishment of all desires') Gautama. It is said that a hermit came down from the mountains to see the new heir, and made a prediction. The boy, he declared, would either become a mighty king and rule the world, or a wandering saint who would set it free. This prophecy had great significance for the prince's upbringing: the king was to do all in his power to prevent his son from embracing the life of a hermit. To keep him happy, the king placed every form of pleasure at his son's disposal, but also subjected him to strict military training. He hired teachers to educate the prince in all the knowledge of the age; he was expected to be the complete man – the warrior-king.

On the outward journey we stopped at Piparava, one of the places archaeologists think may have been Kapilavastu, the capital of the kingdom. It lies very close to the Nepalese border, and there is a brick *stupa* (memorial monument) where, between 1898 and 1971, various finds were made, including precious stones and votive terracotta artefacts. Amongst the latter was a small oval reliquary urn containing bones and bearing an inscription suggesting that these belonged to the Buddha. Tests dated them, in fact, to the fifth century BCE. A little further off, they found what they thought might be the palace; only the brick foundations remained, since the rest of the building, originally two storeys high, had been made of wood. Traces of twenty or so rooms were visible, including a kitchen, a room for bathing, and a stable-block for elephants and horses. According to the Buddha's own words, there should have been at least three palaces:

'Yes, monks, I was brought up in the greatest refinement. Too many, perhaps, were the blessings I enjoyed. I had three pools all for my personal delight; in one there bloomed blue lotuses, in another white lotuses, and in the third red lotuses. I anointed my body with no lotion save sandalwood oil from Varanasi; my clothes too, my coat, my tunic and my trousers, all came from Varanasi. Day and night, servants fanned me lest the flies and other insects torment me, so that the dust would not touch me or disturb my pleasure. I owned three palaces: one for the summer, one for the winter, and one for the *rainy season. During all four months of the rains, I remained inside the monsoon palace, never passing its doors; everywhere I was accompanied by courtesans who danced and played music, sang, and looked to my pleasure without cease. For years I had lived a life untouched by care ... And yet, little by little, monks, I realized that this could not last for ever. I realized I could not escape old age and decrepitude. Whenever I saw an old man, I felt downhearted. So, monks, all my pride in my youth and beauty utterly vanished away.*

'When I saw the sick, I realized that I, too, could fall sick at any moment. Again, I was downhearted. And with this knowledge, my pride in my health and my strength utterly vanished away.

'In the end, death comes to all men, great or humble. And when I saw men dying or dead, I felt downhearted. And so, monks, all my pride in my princely life utterly vanished away.'

The young prince was married to a woman called Yasodhara, from a neighbouring clan. When he was twenty-nine, his wife gave birth to their only child, Rahula. But the birth brought him no peace. Indeed, his torment increased.

Haunted by the notion that he was chained to this world – the meaning of which he yearned to understand – Siddhartha left the palace one night with his white horse and one serving-man. After some distance, the prince ordered his man to lead the horse home and he sent with him his final farewells. He cut off his long hair, exchanged his silken garments for the coarse robes of a monk, and set off, alone, in the direction of the south.

For us, the attempt to retrace the wanderings of the 'Lord Buddha' in that autumn season – the driest and best – ends here. Tired but happy, we would press on to the valley of Kathmandu where, at every street corner, we would be met by those gently smiling faces and those gestures (*mudras*) which ceaselessly seemed to remind us to 'consider the present moment'. For Buddha himself said:

'Things are preceded by the spirit, dominated by the spirit, composed of the spirit. If we act or speak with a spirit that is corrupt, grief will follow us as the wheel follows the foot of the draught-ox. If we act with a spirit that is pure, then happiness will follow us, like the shadow that never leaves our side ...'

Meanwhile, a chorus of birds is singing, and the reflection of the tree lies in the sky-blue mirror of the water.

But what did he do during those first years of his wanderings? We must assume that the life of a mendicant was in itself a harsh enough apprenticeship for a man accustomed to such comforts as few of his time enjoyed. Sleeping in the open air and on the hard ground, living on scraps of food, rubbing shoulders continually with the common folk – all this was more than enough to open the prince's eyes to the complex reality of human existence. And in this, the most religious country in the world, the young man who had had to learn the *Vedas* from his teachers was soon being approached by *sadhus* in search of eternal truths.

From his conversations with the *sadhus*, the young Gautama was perhaps already learning yogic techniques, but also names – names of famous ascetics that he would later visit. He also learnt the name of a place: Varanasi, the holiest of all holy cities, and the meeting place of the yogis. The chronicles have recorded the names of three ascetics whom he visited; he later became the disciple of each in turn, only to leave them after he had acquired their knowledge. They were Bhagava, Arada Kalama and Udraka

Ramaputra. We need only recall here the episode of his meeting with Arada Kalama, the spiritual head of an aboriginal tribe, as it is described in the *Sarvastivadin Sutra:*

*'I went to see Arada Kalama and said to him: "Arada, I wish to practise pure conduct (*brahmacharya*) according to the doctrine (dharma). Is it possible?" Arada replied to me: "O Venerable One, it is not impossible for me. If you wish to practise it, then practise it." I asked further: "O Arada, this doctrine, do you know it for yourself, do you recognize it for yourself, can you see it with your own eyes?" Arada replied: "O Venerable One, having utterly passed beyond the infinite realm of consciousness (*vijnananantyayatana*), having reached the domain of no-thingness (*akincanyayatana*), I now reside there. That is why I know this doctrine for myself, why I recognize it for myself, why I see it with my own eyes."*

*Then a thought came to me: "Arada is not the only one to possess this faith (*sraddha*); I, too, possess this faith. Arada is not the only one to possess this energy (*virya*); I too possess this energy. Arada is not the only one to possess this wisdom (*prajna*); I, too, possess this wisdom. Arada knows this doctrine for himself, recognizes it* for himself, sees it with his own eyes. Because I desire to see this doctrine with my own eyes, I shall go and live alone, apart from other men, in a deserted and tranquil place; with thoughts (citta) devoid of distractions (apramatta), I will cultivate this doctrine and practise it zealously and diligently."

'So I lived alone, separated from other men, in a deserted and tranquil place; with thoughts devoid of distractions, I cultivated this doctrine zealously and diligently, and soon came to see it with my own eyes. Having seen this doctrine with my own eyes, I returned once more to Arada Kalama and asked him: "Arada, this doctrine that you know for yourself, that you recognize for yourself, that you see with your own eyes, is it really this: having passed beyond the infinite realm of consciousness, having reached the realm of no-thingness, you reside there?" Arada Kalama replied: "O Venerable One, the doctrine that I know for myself, that I recognize for myself, that I see with my own eyes, is indeed this: having passed the infinite realm of consciousness and reached the domain of no-thingness, I reside there." And he added: "O Venerable One, do you really see this doctrine with your own eyes, as I do?" "Even as you do, with my own eyes, I

*truly see this doctrine." "O Venerable One, come, let us
share the leadership of this band of disciples."*

*'So it was that Arada installed me in the master's
place, made me his equal, and bestowed upon me the
greatest honours, the richest gifts, and every possible
blessing. But this thought remained with me: "This
doctrine does not lead to Knowledge (jnana), it does not
lead to Awakening (bodhi), it does not lead to Extinction
(nirvana)."'*

We are bound to wonder how many times the
Buddha abandoned his masters like this, after learning the
techniques of yoga and *pranayama* (control of the
breathing), the purification rituals, the principles of
philosophy, and the forms of meditation which led him to
experience a variety of psychic states – including, on this
occasion, the total absence of thought. The *sutras* do not tell
us, but we can at least surmise that these fleeting
encounters were very numerous. Disappointed by the
religious teaching of his day and still uncertain about his
future path, the young man had decided to pursue his quest
in solitude. Leaving Varanasi, he made for the south-west,
towards what is now Bihar.

AWAKENING

Patna~*Pataliputra*

The heat is oppressive. Night falls on a town swathed in mist and smoke and on stalls lit by candles, oil-lamps and torches – countless little lights flickering amid swarms of insects. There are crowds on the streets, their dark eyes shining; making your way to your destination is like swimming breast-stroke through a sea of tattered clothing, dark shapes and inquisitive faces. Some of these people display an extraordinary nobility, like the fifteen-year-old girl in her ragged sari, carrying her baby on her hip with a dignity that tugs at your heart, the beauty of her face radiating through the half-light. Everywhere, life teems amid dirt and dilapidation; strangely though, the human presences seem to have a greater impact on us here than anywhere else. The air is vibrant with a surreal music: the ceaseless tinkling bells of the town's rickshaws. The noise is as much a homage to the night as a warning to passers-by. Here in India, reality is cloaked in mystery and the two constantly blend together, both in waking and in dreaming.

Paris is far away – little of the city remains with me in what has become my world for the duration of this trip: the faces and smiles of women and a fleeting sense of their presence, odd memories which come to haunt the secret places of my brain. (This is so especially at night, as is the way with ghosts – an influx of electrical stimuli transmitted along the nerves of the brain, images you can watch like a film. Sometimes, for a fraction of a moment, you feel a sudden urge to speak to them.)

We are now in Bihar, the poorest, most underprivileged region of the subcontinent. It is three o'clock in the morning. A cricket chirps outside the window; someone is coughing in the room next door. Far away, accompanied by the sporadic barking of dogs, the sound of chanting floats up to the morning sky.

Vaisali~*Vesali*

Today, as with every day during this expedition, we're up at five o'clock to leave at the crack of dawn and make the most of the day. It's not wise to travel at night because of possible breakdowns (few vehicles have headlamps) and also because of *dacoits*, the highway robbers who infest these regions and do not hesitate to hold large farms and villages to ransom.

In the entrance hall of the rest-house stands a massive Buddha made of black stone. Glistening with oil, his back straight, his hands spread palm-upwards, one upon the other and linked thumb-tip to thumb-tip, he has been captured by the sculptor in the perfect meditational posture known in Zen as *zazen*. This is the very same posture the real

Buddha adopted during his Enlightenment, or Awakening, as I prefer to call it.

We leave for Vaisali. With only an inch to spare, our jeep manages to squeeze onto a hulk of a ferry overloaded with trucks. We pull out onto the Ganges – the river is immense, red in the rising sun. Whole families are washing themselves on the muddy banks, singing, shouting, plunging in and out of the water, and eagerly greeting the fiery disc as it clears the horizon. There is a constant procession of boats. Some are driven by paddlewheels. Others are ancient craft with torn square sails, and laden with cargo; men struggle along the towpath, hauling them hour after hour on the journey to port.

Why are we going to Vaisali? Because the Buddha often came to preach and seek converts in this region, which was then the site of a flourishing civilization – as was all of Bihar 2,400 years ago. The rare ruins to be found are half-buried, and remind us that people and civilizations are but handfuls of dust.

Dry land again. The narrow road ahead, like the pine trees, looks neither old nor modern. Were it not for the thin strip of bitumen, the wayside scenes could be the same ones that greeted a traveller thousands of years ago; houses of mud and straw, wooden ploughs drawn by a pair of oxen, women with water-pots on their heads, children playing in the shade of spreading trees ... The only difference is the occasional spluttering roar of a bus or lorry passing by in a cloud of exhaust fumes.

Here, nature transcends time. On foot, we plunge deep into the wilderness, finally reaching Asoka's monument. It is the only one to survive intact of all those erected by the famous emperor at important points on the Awakened One's route. They were also, of course, marking his own modest progress! There it stands, crowned by its haughty lion gazing to the north-west. It was from here, where a ruined *stupa* still commemorates his arrival, that the Buddha left the rich kingdoms of Bihar to embrace death beneath the Himalayas. All around us, nature has reasserted her rights and, on the return journey, we are once more struck by how human beings and animals manage to coexist in perfect harmony: the birds which alight within touching distance; cows, dogs, goats, buffaloes; old folk and inquisitive children; exquisite young women and girls in their multi-coloured saris; men with faces devoid of expression but which seldom fail to light up at the first sign of a smile. Our feet plod on through the yellow dust of the track.

Then, at nightfall, there is the nightmarish reloading of the ferry for the return crossing: using only the light of our headlamps, fifteen-ton vehicles are manoeuvred on to the deck with a roar of motors and a chorus of shouts and yells.

The crossing is made under a sky ablaze with stars. We lie on the warm bonnet of the jeep, while the Ganges laps against the ferry's hull. On board there is total silence. All of us on deck share these moments of spiritual fulfilment on the sacred river – moments when neither race, class nor age count any longer, all submerged beneath our common humanity.

Patna~*Pataliputra*

Dawn. Already we are tramping along the riverbank. We meet some ascetic *sadhus*, their hair all matted, their bodies covered with ashes. After an hour's walk by the water's edge we arrive at the cremation ground where we spend another three hours watching the bodies undergoing the last rites before being burned. They usually arrive tied to rickshaws, stiff and white in their shrouds, sometimes wrapped in a length of costly material which is removed before the fire is lit. Do the mourners realize we are trying to be respectful? In any case, none of the Hindus show any objection to our presence in this place where life and death are inseparable.

Squatting down on the bare sand, the closest relative

of the deceased is shaved. Then the head of the corpse is uncovered and a little rice placed between his teeth; this, one ritual among many, represents his last meal. Now the assistants – members of the very lowest caste – place the body on the pile of big logs, cover it again and light some of the straw. The fire takes hold eagerly. Feet stick out of the flames, flesh liquefies and then falls away. We glimpse bones – startlingly white. They soon snap apart and are tossed back on the pyre with the help of a pole.

Several pyres are ablaze like this, in varying stages of consumption. Some are no more than piles of smoking ashes on the riverbank, soon to be cast onto the water. No tears, no wailing, only the disposal of bodies whose souls have passed on. To be born again as who or what, I wonder? The heat from the sun and the flames is intense. A journey into the beyond through the destruction of the body's shell. A Brahmin widower bathes, and performs the ritual gestures beside his wife's pyre. She was old; we glimpsed her face earlier. A kind of priestly mask. Now it must look like nothing at all.

I think of the words of the Buddha:

'I say to you in truth: our bodies – yours and mine –

are subject to one same law, one single destiny. From this
no man shall escape.'

A little further on, processions of men, women and children, their bodies streaming with sweat, are climbing up from the bank to the road with baskets of sand on their heads. It reminds us of some Hollywood epic. No, it is not a dream. Yet, as we set off towards Rajgir, everything is already only a memory.

We arrive at the Tourist Bungalow where we find darkness and chaos. The electricity has broken down. We enjoy a curry dinner (for a change). Finally to bed ... and then, at two o'clock, I have a dreadful attack of dysentery. I get back into bed, feeling totally drained, and collapse panting. I have visions of myself reduced to a skeleton, doubled up in a never-ending agony. A source of profound meditation ... and purification!

Rajgir ~ *Rajagrha*

I just manage to get to sleep when my traveling companion (J.L. Nou) taps at the door. It is time to leave already. The pills have worked, but now and again the stomach-cramps return. Excruciating!

As we set off again it is still night, but hues of pink and blue are appearing on the horizon. In the brightening dawn we climb towards Vulture Peak. Bent double, I reach the top, and immediately take off my shoes to touch the earth with my bare feet. Now I feel better. The view is magnificent: one of those that really do take the breath away, with hills and valleys stretching further than the eye can see. In one place, enormous rocks seem to be jostling for space. From a nearby hilltop comes the harsh, rhythmic music of a drum. (Later we learn that this is a daily ritual – a Japanese monk from a neighbouring Buddhist temple greeting the sunrise.)

The Buddha lived here for years. In this bright and luminous place, he dwelt with his disciples in caves, preaching to the crowds from the rocks, high up where the ruins of a temple now stand. The local rajah offered him a park with a lake – the so-called Bamboo Park – where he could rest during the hot season: this was further down the valley, where there are sulphurous streams with healing properties. Dozens of legends survive; snapshots of a life so passionate and urgent as to be almost beyond belief.

The sun comes over the horizon, filling the valley with radiance.

We are off to Rajgir again. As the car heads towards Bodh-Gaya (Gaya to Hindus), I read the following:

'In truth, monks, seeking what is good, seeking in all directions the place of supreme peace, travelling on foot among the Magadha, little by little I drew near the village of Uruvela, where I found a charming spot, with a lovely wood and a pleasant river. The water was clear and hurried along between gently shelving banks; all around were

villages where I could obtain my food. O monks, this was the thought that came to me: "Delightful, indeed, is this place, this lovely wood and these clear waters hurrying between their gentle banks, these villages all around where I can obtain my food. In truth, this is a good place for a son and heir to contemplate a mighty struggle. Yes, this is a place worthy of a mighty struggle." In truth, monks, I sat down on the self-same spot still thinking: "This is a place for a mighty struggle."'

Bodh-Gaya~*Uruvela*

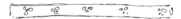

The region is still giving off good vibrations, and the road by the river passes through some magnificent country. Here, the width of the main stream, as it slips between its sandbanks, is over half a mile at least. Both banks are clothed with attractive vegetation; there is a sprinkling of wattle-and-daub villages. The mountains in the distance are not very tall, but their summits are sharp and jagged, breaking up the monotony of the skyline. It is hard to explain what gives a place its atmosphere, but each locality has its own: a combination of energies – from the earth, the plant life, the water and the atmosphere – which creates a unique environment. And, indisputably, some places have a more powerful aura than others; they are more charged with 'energy', though this term is not given to precise definition. It is merely the impression imprinted in a rather confused way on our senses.

So the Buddha installed himself in this spot. Was it in a cave in this mountain, as local legends claim? What we do know is that he undertook a ruthless programme of fasting and what is euphemistically known as 'non-breathing meditation'. A superb sculpture (in Kabul Museum, Afghanistan) depicts him at this point in his life: half-skeleton, half-living man, locked in the struggle to find a state that transcends both life and death.

> 'In truth, O Aggivessana, if I thought "I will touch my spine", it was the skin of my belly I also took hold of, and when I thought "I will touch the skin of my belly", I was also feeling my spine. For, O Aggivessana, I was so wasted away with fasting that the skin of my belly cleaved to my spine.'

At this point, the chronicles go on to tell us of one of his temptations:

'By the side of the broad River Niranjana, I was
struggling with myself, striving unflinchingly to conquer
my servitude, when Namuci approached me. With words
of pity he cloaked his intentions. "How pale and thin you
are; you are close to death, but life has not left you entirely.
Live, Lord, for such is the true path towards merit. Come,
enjoy this blessed life, pour libations on the sacred fires,
and you will gain the world of merit. Why struggle? The
way of struggling is harsh and difficult." As he spoke,
Mara crept up to me.'

And the Supreme One rebuked Mara:

'O Spirit of Evil, cousin of the Thoughtless One, you
seek only to attain your ends. I have no need of merit. Let
Mara speak of merit to those who need it. For I possess
faith and strength, and I have discernment also. This wind
that blows can dry up even the waters of the rivers; so why,
whilst I wage this battle, should it not also dry up my
blood? As the blood dries up, the bile and phlegm are
diminished, and the exhaustion of the flesh appeases the
soul. And I shall be more attentive, more awake, more
single-pointed in my task. For, living as I do, I am

49

beginning to learn that feelings have their limits; the desires of the flesh no longer reach my soul. You see before you a being who is pure. The first squadron of your army is emotion and desire; the second is boredom; hunger and thirst comprise the third; then comes envy, and then laziness and discouragement. The sixth is cowardice, the seventh, doubt. The eighth, finally, is malevolence, combined with stubbornness and perversity. To these are added profit, honours, fame and notoriety gained by evil means, vanity and disparagement. Those are the arms with which evil does battle. Only the brave will find a way to conquer them and attain happiness. Unfurling the victor's banner, I utter my battle-cry: "Better to die fighting than to live with defeat." So, let Mara deploy his forces; I go to meet him. Though all the gods of the universe cannot overthrow his hosts, yet as the stone shatters a coarse clay pot, I will shatter them with my wisdom.'

And, with a kind of fury born of impatience, a ferocious desire to transcend the limits of this bodily shell – the same passion we find later in many a Christian mystic – he continued this merciless asceticism which rendered his flesh 'like the skin of a gourd, bitter and wizened and shrivelled with the wind and heat'.

'I thought: "Each time a monk or a Brahmin has
felt, feels, or will feel the atrocious suffering of struggle, this
may equal my experience, but never surpass it. This
relentless penance has allowed me to reach wisdom, which
is all that is noble in a man."'

But his body, already exhausted by fasting, became
even weaker. He realized that dying, even with an entirely
lucid mind, was not the answer. Was there another way
toward the light?

'I remembered one day in my childhood, when my
father was working in a field and I sat beneath the cool
shade of a flowering tree. Then, secure from all desires of
the flesh, sheltered from barren thoughts, I had my first
experience of meditation, full of the pensiveness and joy
which only solitude affords. I thought: "Could that
experience be the path to the light?" And I knew that it
was indeed the path to the light.
'I thought again: "Why fear such happiness? It is not
linked to the desires of the flesh, nor to useless wealth and

possessions." After this, I no longer feared this path.

'I thought: "It is impossible to reach that state with a body so wasted. Let me then take a little food each day."'

And he went down again to the valley.

It has taken us three hours' walking to reach this mountain cave where the Buddha is said to have lived in meditation. We have been charged by a buffalo in one of the villages and have waded knee-deep three times through a muddy river; our throats are parched, so it's good to taste the green tea offered by a Tibetan monk. He is a member of a Buddhist community which has set up a small temple close by. The master-cave is round, a hollow formed in the rock face which you enter through a tiny opening. Ten feet or so in front, an outcrop completely blocks the view over the valley. What inner voyages of exploration went on here, I wonder, in this cavern cut off from the world, before the day came when the Buddha emerged exhausted, and returned to the valley with its trees and its thronging life?

Next door is the temple and its terrifying divinities. When the doors open, a strange form of energy seems to seize upon my body. Am I just reacting to those cruel and gruesome figures meant to represent our passions?

As you leave, you have to sign the visitors' book. Opposite your signature, you fill in, of course, the amount of your donation – the monks haven't forgotten their business sense!

We climb down again and, for the first time since we arrived in the country, the dogs chase after us with a flurry of barks. I feel the effect of a strange force; perhaps I have forgotten to carry out some ritual to disperse it – burning incense, for example. True temples are centres of energy, both good and bad; they reflect energy like mirrors. Lead only becomes gold with secret rituals and arcane rites! These temples are mysterious places, where the forces of nature, earth and man come together: physical and psychical auras which imprint themselves on the memory of plants and stones. Troubled, I concentrate on what is before my eyes; I feel deep down something like a sense of unease. As I cross a river, using a simple tree-trunk as a bridge, the disagreeable feeling vanishes, dispelled perhaps by my momentary concentration on something difficult. Feeling calmer, I sit down on the bank and look about. A little mannikin of a monkey suddenly appears and squats in the middle of the trunk, chewing on his twig-toothbrush. A timeless moment, pregnant with meaning. The sun, right above our heads, beats down hard; we arrive, hot, bothered and tired, at Bodh-Gaya.

A shower, a meal in a cool room in the rest-house: curried chicken with chapattis dipped in sauce.

Afternoon, and our route is through the countryside, with its forests and rice paddies. The people we meet, their gestures, the fields: all is harmony. An illusion? No, these people lack everything, but they possess that one essential of harmony. Another sandy river crossed; more primitive villages. In one of them is a mound marking the spot where the Buddha took his first food: he had barely decided to end his futile fast when he was offered some milk and rice by Sujata, a woman who had just given birth. This was where he regained his strength, where his energy was reawakened amid the grandeur of the landscape. One of the groves in the distance is said to be the famous one where he conceived the idea of the Middle Way. Worn out by fasting, leaning against a tree, he heard a teacher of music talking to his pupils in a nearby grove:

'If the strings of the lute are too taut, they snap or emit discordant notes. Too slack, and the sound is no longer right.

The instrument must be exactly in tune to produce its music.'

A sublime metaphor of the creativity which is mankind's gift. Two Sri-Lankan monks in orange robes pass nearby; greetings and smiles. Back over the river once more. Waiting for the sun to go down, I lean against a tree, shut my eyes and – is this real? – melt into the universe and all its sounds.

When the Bodhisattva had regained his strength, he betook himself to the edge of the River Niranjana and entered the water. Having bathed his body, he left the water, climbed on to the bank and went to a tree of his choosing. At this moment, not far from the tree, there was a man scything the grass that they call kusa *– holy or blessed. The Bodhisattva went to introduce himself to this man and said: 'I need some grass directly. Can you give me so much?' The other replied: 'Certainly, for I am not a mean man.' Straightaway he gave the Bodhisattva some grass. He took it, went to the foot of the sacred* asvattha *tree, made himself a cushion of grass and sat on it, his body very upright, his mind correct, his thoughts concentrated on what was before him.*

Time now to visit the temple which stands guard over this place of Awakening. A gigantic *stupa* temple surrounded by statues and smaller *stupas* scattered in a vast park. Hordes of chanting pilgrims tour the building, always in a clockwise direction as tradition demands. So many people, yet an enormous sense of peace flows from the place. Behind the temple is the famous tree. Obviously not the same one – yet it is the same, because the present trunk has grown from a shoot of the original. Here is the tranquillity of the Bodhi Tree or 'Root Tree'. Maybe it is the fervour of the crowds, who have been coming here for two thousand years to pay homage to the place where a prince-turned-yogi discovered his truths, sitting for seven days in a row among its roots; maybe the tree, too, has its own source of power. Whatever the reason, this is another place which casts a spell over the visitor.

In this spot, in a moment of sublime intuition beneath the gaze of the Morning Star, the Buddha suddenly became aware, in both mind and body, of the beginning and end of the universe, the cycle of lives and deaths, his past existences, the mystery and complexity of the cosmos, the creation of worlds. He discovered that matter is formed from nothing, that time is infinite but that cycles of time exist; he saw death giving birth to life as darkness brings forth light, and vice versa. The whole physical universe and its laws appeared clearly before him – likewise, the flight of humanity from its true nature – in the frantic search for fame, success and pleasure, people hurtle toward suffering, creating *karma*, the chain of cause and effect which imprisons their souls.

But to understand fully what happened there and the exhausting nature of this meditation, it is important to study how he himself described it later to his disciples.

Among the roots of the tree, already considered sacred, Gautama sat down cross-legged in the lotus position on his grass cushion – also well-known for dispensing beneficial energy – and began the long meditation which was to lead to Awakening. Concentrating on his breathing, he determined not to move from the spot till he had achieved what he was seeking:

'I had this idea: "It is better that I separate my thoughts and make two parts of them. Into one part I shall separate sensual desires and thoughts of malevolence and hurtfulness; into the other, thoughts devoid of desire and malevolence and hurtfulness." With my mind free from

distractions, disciplined, practised, exercised and full of energy, as soon as I experienced the thought of a desire, I said deliberately to myself: "The thought of a desire is being born; it is harmful to oneself, it is harmful to others, it destroys wisdom, troubles and tires one much, and does not lead to Extinction." As soon as I did this, the thought disappeared. Further, as soon as a malevolent or hurtful thought entered my head, I said to myself: "A harmful thought has just been born. It is harmful to oneself, it harms others, and does not lead to Extinction." As soon as I did this, the thought disappeared. Thoughts of desire were born, but I refused to entertain them, I cast them out, I drove them away, I vomited them forth. Why? Because I foresaw the endless evil and harm that would follow them.

'Monks, the mind becomes as the thoughts and reflections that fill it. If a monk continually reflects upon desire, he must abandon this reflection, for his mind will become as his thoughts. And if a monk continually reflects upon malevolence and hurtfulness, he must abandon this reflection, for his mind will become as those thoughts also.

'Then I thought: "If I reflect and ponder for a long time, my body will lose its joy, and my thinking will suffer. It is better therefore that I restrain my thoughts within me;

that my thoughts remain deep inside me and at rest. Being
intent on one purpose, I shall acquire single-pointed
concentration, and my meditations will be unhindered."
Thenceforth I restrained my thoughts within me, I kept
them constantly within me and at rest; I set my mind to a
single purpose, I attained single-pointed concentration and
nothing came to injure my meditations. When a reflection
devoid of desire was born, I gave birth to another reflection
and directed it toward my ideas, I set it amongst my ideas.
And when a reflection devoid of malevolence and
hurtfulness was born, I directed it, too, towards my ideas,
and set it amongst my ideas. Why? Because I saw no
infinity of evil and harmful consequences.'

Starting from his posture which was peaceful but full
of energy, his thoughts perfectly concentrated, he
experienced four stages of meditation.

*'Having divorced myself from sensual desires (*kama*),*
*having divorced myself from unwholesome (*akusala*) things*
*(*dharmas*), having attained the first stage of meditation*
*(*dhyana*), where there is reasoning (*vitakka*) and reflection*
*(*vicara*), born of separation, composed of joy (*piti*) and*

*happiness (sukha), I remained in this state. In truth, O
Aggivessana, this highly agreeable sensation (vedana) arose
within me and persisted, but without taking complete
control of my thoughts (citta). Full of the peace that fell
upon my reasoning and reflection, having reached the
second stage of meditation, comprising inner serenity and
unity of thought, where reasoning and reflection are
absent, and which is born of single-pointed concentration
(samadhi), I remained in that state.*

*In truth, this highly agreeable sensation arose
within me and persisted, but without taking complete
control of my thoughts. Detaching myself from joy, I
remained in that state, dispassionate, attentive and aware;
I felt throughout my body that happiness spoken of by
the saints when they describe themselves as dispassionate,
attentive, and persisting in happiness. Having attained
the third stage of meditation, I remained thus.*

*In truth, O Aggivessana, this highly agreeable
sensation arose within me and persisted, but without
taking complete control of my thoughts. Through the
abandonment of pleasure and pain, through the prior
disappearance of joy and sadness, having attained
the fourth stage of meditation, neither painful nor*

*pleasurable, but comprising dispassion and single-pointed
concentration, I remained in that state.'*

Through these four stages of meditation (the
Fourfold Absorption) which produced a particular psychic
state characterized by intense concentration, Gautama
transformed his mind into a clear mirror. Sitting motionless
for seven whole days, he plunged into a sort of visionary
trance which has been described as follows:

*When the Bodhisattva had reached this single-
pointed concentration, with all restraints cast aside, when
his mind was perfectly pure and without blemish,
malleable and workable, firmly established and immovable,
he saw with his own eyes the Truth concerning previous
existences. He recalled his own previous experiences: one
birth, two births, three births, four, five, ten, twenty, thirty,
forty births, countless hundreds of births, countless
thousands of births, cosmic cycles of creation, cosmic cycles
of destruction, countless cosmic cycles of creation, countless
cosmic cycles of destruction ... And he thought: 'That was
me; once I lived in such-and-such a place, that was my
name, my clan, my caste, I ate food like that, I lived like*

that, I lived so many years, my stay in this world was so long or so short, I experienced such pleasures and such pains. Then I died, and was reborn in such-and-such a place. I died again, and was reborn over there. I died again, and was reborn here.' And so he learnt the facts of innumerable previous existences in all their shapes and forms. When the Bodhisattva acquired the first knowledge during the first watch of the night, ignorance ceased and knowledge appeared, the darkness parted and light shone forth – that is, the all-pervading vision of previous existences. Why? Because of his energy and his freedom from distractions.

*When the Bodhisattva had focused his thoughts using single-pointed concentration (*samadhi*) and rendered his mind perfectly pure and free of blemish and cast off every restraint, when he had completely removed every stain from his mind and made it malleable and workable, fixed and immovable, he learnt of the births and deaths of men. Thanks to the perfect purity of the divine eye, he saw the Truth concerning the births and deaths of men, handsome or ugly, men of good or evil destiny, illustrious or humble. According to their conduct, he knew them entirely. Examining them for himself, he knew that men*

whose conduct was evil, whose words were reprehensible,
whose opinions were false, who criticized and denigrated
the saints, who acted on evil advice, these – upon the
destruction of their bodies at the ending of their lives – fell
into the infernal regions, amongst the animals and starving
ghosts. He saw, too, that those whose conduct was good,
whose words were good, whose opinions were correct, who
neither criticized nor denigrated the saints, who acted on
good advice, these – upon the destruction of their bodies at
the ending of their lives – would be reborn either in heaven
or amongst men. And, thanks to the perfect purity of the
divine eye, he saw that men are born and die according to
their conduct. This is what is called the second knowledge,
which the Bodhisattva acquired during the middle watch of
the night. His ignorance ceased and knowledge appeared,
the darkness parted and light shone forth; that is, the light
of the divine eye which sees the works of men. Why?
Because of his energy and his single-pointed concentration.

When the Bodhisattva had acquired a mind thus
concentrated and perfectly pure, free from blemish,
malleable and workable, which remained firm and
immovable in its place, he acquired the knowledge of the
destruction of impure influences. His thoughts being intent

*upon receiving knowledge of the destruction of impure
influences, he then came to know the reality of suffering,
came to know the reality of the cessation of suffering. And,
on obtaining the holy virtues, he knew them in reality. He
knew the origin of impurities, the cessation of impurities,
and the Way that leads to the cessation of impurities; he
knew these things in reality. Having done this, he knew in
this manner, lived in this manner. His mind was delivered
from the impurity of desire, his mind was delivered from
the impurity of existence, his mind was delivered from the
impurity of ignorance. Thus he obtained the knowledge of
deliverance, and thought: 'For me, there is no more rebirth.
I have attained purity of conduct; my task is accomplished.
I shall not be born again.' This is what is called the third
knowledge, which the Bodhisattva obtained during the
final watch of the night. Ignorance ceased and wisdom
appeared; the darkness parted and light shone forth, the
light that issues from the cessation of impurities. Why?
Because arhat, the Tathagata – perfectly and completely
enlightened – produced this wisdom, he obtained pure and
perfect deliverance.*

Gautama had achieved Buddhahood. And the tree

which sheltered him would henceforth be known as the Bodhi Tree and as the Tree of the Root of Knowledge. The perpetual restlessness and transformation of existence, as well as the law of causality which acts upon every being, appeared to him in a succession of states of altered consciousness, each more far-reaching than the preceding, and which revealed to him the secrets of suffering, of the cause of suffering, of the cessation of suffering, and of the Way which leads to the cessation of suffering. And legend tells us that, by the light of the Morning Star, as night began to melt into the dawn, the Buddha returned to normal consciousness. He discovered himself just sitting there, breathing in the fresh air and enjoying the moment to the full in what we would call 'real time'.

He had come to understand the twelve links in the chain of cause and effect known as the conditional nexus or theory of dependent origination.

Events or phenomena occur due to some anterior cause. If the anterior cause ceases, what has been brought into being also ceases. That is to say:

1   *ignorance* gives rise to
2   *volitional action*, which in turn gives rise to

3   *conditioned consciousness,* which in turn gives rise to

4   *name and form,* which in turn give rise to

5   *the six spheres of the senses,* which in turn give rise to

6   *sensory impressions,* which in turn give rise to

7   *feelings,* which in turn give rise to

8   *cravings,* which in turn give rise to

9   *attachments,* which in turn give rise to

10 *becoming,* which in turn gives rise to

11 *birth,* which in turn gives rise to

12 *death,* including old age, sorrow, illness, suffering
    and pain.

If ignorance ceases, volitional actions cease. If volitional actions cease, conditioned consciousness ceases. If conditioned consciousness ceases, name and form cease. If name and form cease, the six spheres of the senses cease. If the six spheres of the senses cease, sensory impressions cease. If sensory impressions cease, feelings cease. If feelings cease, cravings cease. If cravings cease, attachments cease. If attachments cease, becoming ceases. If becoming ceases, birth ceases. If birth ceases, death and old age cease, together with sorrow, illness and pain.

As soon as the Buddha had acquired this knowledge,

he uttered these stanzas:

> 'All things, in truth, are born of cause and effect.
> If, in his first meditation,
> The Brahmin understands this law,
> He may reject all doubts,
> He may reject all suffering.

> 'All things, in truth, are born of cause and effect.
> The Brahmin who, in his first meditation,
> Disperses the darkness within him,
> He is like the sun
> That climbs to the spaces of heaven.'

But his profound waking meditation was, in fact, to last forty-nine days, in different places.

> *After taking the milk and rice which Sujata brought him, the Buddha moved from the foot of the Tree of Awakening to the Goatherd's Banyan Tree; there he sat down, legs crossed, and remained for seven more days, savouring the joy of his emancipation.*
> *Then, as it happened, a certain discontented*

*Brahmin approached the Blessed One. At first, he merely indulged in polite conversation, but then he went and stood apart, saying: 'Tell me, Gautama my friend, what does it mean to be a Brahmin? And what are his duties?' Then the Blessed One exclaimed: 'The Brahmin who makes it a rule to drive away evil, without grumbling, who is free from impurities, master of himself; who has attained supreme wisdom and accomplished pure conduct (*brahmacharya*); that man may lawfully pronounce the words of Brahma, for he has no pride in this world.'*

After seven days, the Blessed One, having emerged from his meditation, left the foot of the Goatherd's Banyan Tree for the Mucalinda Tree. He sat at the foot of the Mucalinda Tree, legs crossed, for seven whole days, savouring the joy of his emancipation.

In truth, at this moment, a great cloud of rain appeared, and for seven days the weather was wet and cold, windy and dark. Then, in truth, the Serpent King of the Naga, Mucalinda, leaving his own abode, came to the Goatherd's Banyan. He wrapped the body of the Blessed One in his sevenfold coils, and spread his great hood above the head of the Blessed One, and remained there thinking: 'Let not the Blessed One be cold, let not the Blessed One be

hot, let the Blessed One be protected from the mosquitoes, from the wind, from the heat and fierce creeping things.'
Then in truth, at the end of the seven days, seeing that the sky was clear and without clouds, having unwound his coils from the body of the Blessed One, having abandoned his proper form, having magically assumed the shape of a young man, he stood upright before the Blessed One, greeting him with hands joined.

Then the Blessed One, seeing this, exclaimed: 'Pleasant is solitude for him who is satisfied, and has heard the doctrine and sees all things clearly. Pleasant in this world is the absence of malevolence, the mastery of self amidst the living.

'Not to torment the world, that is pleasant. To show goodness and kindness to all men, that too is a pleasant thing.

'It is pleasant to be detached from the world. To leave behind the desire for fame and success, that is a pleasant thing. But to have conquered pride in self, that is the greatest blessing of all.'

The Posture of the Awakened One

A few comments. During these seven-day meditations, the Buddha chose a different tree every time, as if he wanted to experience each one's energy. Indeed, the *sutras* all speak of the fact that each tree possesses a divinity, an essence, an individual existence with which, under certain conditions, man can communicate. Even today, despite our estrangement from nature, there are many who have experienced states of consciousness, albeit subjective ones, in which they have communicated with plant life. We now know, as a result of various experiments, that plants 'feel' not only physical actions – when we water them or cut a leaf or flower – but also intended actions: 'I am going to cut off this leaf,' we think – and the plant reacts. This we can prove using a polygraph connected to the plant. Plants also give off energy; by the process of photosynthesis, of course, but also by their mere presence. Lean against a lime tree or a willow and you will fall asleep; against an oak, and your whole being will feel reinvigorated. So, if the *sutras* speak with such insistence of his choice of different trees, it is because the Buddha, with his hyper-developed perception, felt the constant need to examine and test these auras. Or, perhaps, he was just following his instincts.

This reminds me of the very fine passage describing how, just before his Awakening, he decided to conquer fear:

'Whilst I was staying in a hermitage, when the branches of the trees were broken, when birds or animals ran away in flight, then I thought, "The forest is greatly afraid." And again, I thought, "If fear and terror return, I will seek out a way to prevent them returning anew. If fear and terror assail me as I walk, without taking the time to sit or lie down, I will strive to drive away this fear and this terror, and only then will I sit down ... If fear and terror assail me as I am sitting, without taking the time to start walking, I will strive to drive away this fear and this

terror, and only then will I start to walk."'

Furthermore, the Buddha's revelations came to him with the aid of a posture which was called *raja-yoga*: the practitioner sat in the lotus position, with legs crossed and back erect, remaining motionless for a considerable period. Then, quite naturally, but still aware of what was happening, he was gradually liberated from infiltrations of desire, sensuality, joy and sadness. So his mind would become

> *'single-pointed, purified, reformed, free from impurities, free from sin, malleable and workable, firm and devoid of vacillation'.*

This is the same posture practised now under the name of *zazen*. Let's take a look at it (see my *Techniques de Méditation*, Albin Michel, Paris). First, sit down in the centre of the *zaful* (round cushion). Now cross your legs in the lotus or half-lotus position. Push firmly with your knees against the ground. Arch your spine at the fifth lumbar vertebra. Keeping your upper back and the back of your neck straight, pull in your chin. Align your nose vertically above your navel. Place your left hand in your right (palms upward), in your lap, thumb-tip to thumb-tip, and keep them horizontal. If they form a depression, you will feel tired and sleepy; if they point upwards, your mood will become excited. The shoulders will slope naturally. Keep the tip of your tongue against your palate. The eyes should be half-closed, gently focused on – but not staring at – a point three feet or so in front of you. Your breathing should be calm and soundless. Breathe out as slowly and for as long as you can: there should be a powerful effort from just below the navel in the zone known as *hara* ('ocean of energy', sometimes also called *kikai tanden*). This is the human centre of gravity. You will find that you inhale without making any effort. Concentrate completely on your posture and breathing. Neither encourage nor reject thoughts, images or any mental processes: let them pass by like clouds in the sky. Think without thoughts; pass to the state beyond thought (*hi-shiryo*). Let your own mind be an empty mirror: from the depths of silence, immortal mind will surface.

According to Zen Master, Deshimaru, the following psycho-physiological results of this posture will be observed. The circulation in the brain is considerably improved. The cortex is tranquillized, and the conscious flow of thought arrested, while the flow of blood is better directed towards the deep layers of the brain. The blood-supply of these layers increased, they awaken from a semi-dormant state, and their activity produces an impression of well-being, serenity and calm, approaching a profound sleep, though the practitioner is still awake. The nervous system is relaxed, the 'primitive' part of the brain fully active. The practitioner is highly receptive, aware to the highest possible degree, throughout every cell of his body. Unconsciously, he thinks with his body – all duality, all contradiction is dispersed in the energy generated by the posture. Primitive peoples have maintained a very high level of activity in the lowest parts of the brain. In the development of our civilisation, we have educated and refined our intellects to such a state of sophistication that the force, intuition and wisdom associated with these areas has been lost. This is exactly why this posture represents an inestimable treasure for modern man – at least, if he has the eyes to see and ears to hear. Through the regular practice of *zazen*, he has the opportunity to renew himself by returning to the sources of life. He can reach back to the original condition of body and soul (which are indivisible) by grasping existence at its very roots.

The Buddha understood that meditation should not lead to the obstruction of thought and mental processes; rather, by concentrating on the posture, the practitioner should 'pass from thought to non-thought, and from non-thought to thought'. This is the only way in which the psyche and its 'packaging' – the body – can become the mirror of ourselves.

The Buddha therefore continued his sessions for forty-nine days, under different trees. Under one of them (a rose-apple), some merchants came to visit him, bringing him barley gruel and a ball of honey for refreshment. He gave them instruction, concluding as follows:

'Amongst creatures with two legs, go in peace; amongst creatures with four legs, go in peace. May you have peace as you come; may you have peace as you go ...'

The *sutras* tell us that the food left for him gave rise to 'a flatulence in his abdomen, which was very painful'. Then the spirit of a nearby tree (a *myrobalan*) advised him to eat some of its fruit to relieve his suffering. The Buddha ate, imparting his wisdom to the tree at the same time. Naturally, all these plants were to become part of the extensive mythology which grew up around him.

He then returned and spent yet another week under the Bodhi Tree before going to the village of Uruvela (Bodh-Gaya) and offering instruction to his first benefactress, Sujata, and her family. He now found himself meditating on how to make the best use of his discovery. In the temple courtyard, you can see a series of cylinders made of stones indicating the area where the Buddha is said to have paced back and forth as he considered his dilemma. (Some say that his pacing about in the courtyard was the origin of a Zen practice known as *kinhin*: the practitioner walks in an intense state of concentration, each step coinciding with the final exhalation of a breath.) He then went and sat cross-legged under another tree, and experienced these thoughts:

'This doctrine which I have acquired is very profound, difficult to arrive at, peaceful, benevolent and subtle. It is attainable only by the wisest; the foolish can never practise it. Human beings have different opinions, different amounts of patience, different desires, different ways of living, rely on different opinions, and are happy hiding themselves away like animals in their lairs and dens. And

*since they hide away like this, the law of cause and effect
is hard for them to understand. Besides, there is another
state which is very deep and hard to comprehend: the
cessation of desire, the extinction of cravings – nirvana.
This condition is difficult to acquire; if now I wish to preach
this doctrine and others reject it, I will feel weariness,
exhaustion and pain.'*

Legend has it that this induced the King of the Gods,
Brahma, to intervene and change the Buddha's mind.

*'The world is greatly afflicted with ruin and
destruction. The Tathagata has today acquired this Good
Teaching. Why does he remain silent so that the world
cannot hear it?'*

This episode throws light on both the Buddha's
misgivings and the use of mythology to personify what the
ancients termed 'divine inspiration', introducing a god into
the equation. This is hardly surprising; we are merely
observing a feature common to all new beliefs which
borrow elements of established religions with the aim of
attracting converts. The fact that Brahma, the supreme god

of Hinduism, approached the Buddha with respect and persuaded him to change his mind, could not fail to produce a favourable impression. It is a case of myth being superimposed upon truth. None the less, the Buddha

looked into the deepest minds of men, seeing who was wise and who was foolish. Some fear the three evil destinies that await them, others may receive this doctrine that resembles the ocean. Others still, like lotus buds growing in a muddy place, have raised themselves above the water, or if they have not yet grown out of the water, they are not soiled.

He then uttered these stanzas:

'Before, fearing to exhaust myself in vain,
I did not preach the deepest wisdom.

Now let the gates of immortality be opened,
That all men may hear and know the Truth.'

His doubts overcome, the Buddha decided to make the first announcement of his discoveries to two of his former masters, Arada Kalama and Udraka Ramaputra. But they were both now dead. Then he thought of five travelling companions who had parted company with him one day, and decided to go to Varanasi in search of them. He was now some thirty-six years old and about to set out upon the life of wandering and preaching which continued till his very last breath, some forty-five years later.

With this decision, he took his first steps on the road to fame. Few figures have had such an influence on the history of mankind.

THE WHEEL OF
THE TEACHING

Varanasi

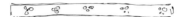

We sit down and collect our thoughts one last time before leaving. We are in the enclosure of the giant *stupa*, under the shade of the Bodhi Tree. The whole place exudes peace ...

Off again. This time to Varanasi along the Grand Trunk Road; we keep our thirst at bay with frequent cups of milky tea and our mouths fresh by chewing betel leaves. At dusk, we come across a scene resembling something out of Dante's *Inferno*. Hundreds of trucks are backed up in queues at a toll; no matter which way you turn you cannot escape them. Indescribable; a sort of satanic dodgems. We get there in the end, and after the third shower, the water finally runs off clean.

Dawn, and we are already at the *ghats* in Varanasi, the most sacred of all sacred cities. Beginning with the *ghat* at the most northerly end of the town, we stroll back along the banks of the Ganges and watch the terracotta lamps floating down the current. Circles of women are performing their rituals, their voices lifted in chanting and prayer. I sit down by a group of them; unresisting, I let their invocations lull me into a sort of meditation. At the same time, I stare at the sun rising once more over the earth and bringing light to humanity – a race of insects, insignificant, like every other creature. Here, self is humbled and acknowledges its kinship with the pulsating infinity of forms which we call life. Yogis are doing their exercises; but I wonder if they remember what the Buddha said:

> *'A man may go naked and let his hair grow matted,*
> *he may cover his body with mud and prostrate himself. But*
> *if he has not overcome his doubts, he will not be purified.'*

Merely a thought. I am making no judgements; I still have my own doubts, certainly. It was here that the Buddha, over the course of some years, disciplined his body and learnt the full range of his techniques before moving on to the cave and the tree, and continuing his travels. He returned to this place after his Awakening. We spend the afternoon sitting in different corners of Sarnath, in the Deer Park, where there are still a few deer left, behind fences. This was where the Buddha preached his first sermon and set in motion the Wheel of the Teaching – the medicine of the soul. The Buddha-nature lies within us all; it is up to us to discover it.

'If a man has conquered a thousand thousand in battle, but another has conquered himself, then the greater victor is the man who has conquered self.'

Tomorrow we will be involved in the celebration of Diwali – the Indian New Year – and the ritual purification through fire conducted by a group of Brahmins: the Lakshmi Puja. We will also take part in the preliminary rites of a Kali Puja and follow the procession carrying the statue of the black goddess to the Ganges. There, after another ceremony, in which all the bad *karma* of the participants is transferred to the image, it is thrown into the water for purification.

Sarnath~*Isipatana*

Back at Sarnath. It is delightful sitting among the various ruins, including the cell where the Buddha is said to have lived. The giant *stupa* watches over the place, dwarfing everything – majestic. An abundance of flowers and birds; groups of people strolling about, looking very relaxed.

The arrival of the Awakened One centuries ago can be reconstructed something like this:

On the highway, between Gaya and the Bodhi Tree,
he met the ascetic, Upaka, who stopped him and said:
'Master, you appear serene. You seem in good spirits

*and full of energy. Who is your guru? What does he
teach you?'*

*And the Buddha replied: 'I have journeyed to the
very end and conquered myself. No chains bind me now. I
have applied myself to the destruction of all desire, and my
wisdom has set me free. You ask who is my teacher? I am
the Awakened One. My spirit has found peace and serenity.
I am going to Varanasi to set in motion the Wheel of the
Teaching. In this blind world, I will cause the voice of
immortality to be heard.'*

*The Blessed One pursued his way and arrived at
the Deer Park. He went to where the five ascetics were
living. When they saw him in the distance, they consulted
together.*

*'Here comes the monk, Gautama. He has neglected
the mortification of the flesh. He does not deserve to be
greeted; we ought not to rise to welcome him. None the
less, we will offer him a place to sit, if he wishes to sit down.'*

*As the Awakened One drew nearer, they found it
hard to persist in their resolution and rose to greet him.
One took his bowl and his robes; another prepared a seat
for him whilst water was fetched so he could wash his feet.*

The Blessed One sat down and washed his feet. They

spoke to him as a friend and called him by his name.

Then he said to them:

'Monks, if you follow my teaching, you will soon attain knowledge by yourselves. Whosoever sanctifies this earthly life shall receive this reward. Therefore let the uninitiated abandon their ordinary lives; let them take up the life of a monk.'

The five monks answered:

'O friend Gautama, if the mortifying of the flesh and penances did not allow you to attain the highest states of enlightenment, nor even a higher state than before, could you in truth, by abandoning all efforts, attain to a higher state, much less to the highest of all?'

Then the Buddha explained:

'Monks, whoever walks in the Way does not enjoy luxury or riches; he has not abandoned all perseverance. He has acquired salvation and perfect Awakening.'

At this they pricked up their ears and were ready to listen. So he preached to the five monks the words which were the first turning of the Wheel of the Teaching.

'Monks, there are two extremes to be avoided by whoever renounces a life of desire. One is luxury and the pleasures of life, it is the expression of triviality and

insignificance, and is accompanied by suffering. The other
is the mortification of the flesh, which is full of pain; this,
too, is accompanied by suffering.

'Monks, it is by avoiding these two extremes that
whoever walks along the Path reaches the Middle Way,
which is the route to clear-sightedness, which awakens
wisdom and leads to the appeasement of the mind, to the
highest form of knowledge, to supreme Awakening and to
emancipation.

'How is this Middle Way reached by whoever walks
in the proper Path? It is by none other than the Noble
Eightfold Path composed of perfect view, perfect resolve,
perfect speech, perfect conduct, perfect livelihood, perfect
effort, perfect mindfulness, perfect concentration.

'This is the Noble Truth of Suffering: birth itself is
suffering, old age is suffering, sickness is suffering, death
is suffering, all that is linked with absence of pleasure is
suffering; so, too, the loss of dear ones is suffering, the
unfulfilment of desire is suffering. In short, the five
aggregates (matter, sensation, perception, mental
formations and consciousness) which constitute our
mortality, are all the cause of suffering.

'This is the Noble Truth of the Origin of Suffering:

the cause of rebirth is insatiable desire. Desire seeks pleasure everywhere; it is the cravings of the senses, the cravings for existence and extinction.

'This is the Noble Truth of the Cessation of Suffering: the utter cessation of, and detachment from, these insatiable desires.

'The Noble Truth Leading to the Cessation of Suffering is the Noble Eightfold Path: perfect view, perfect resolve, perfect speech, perfect conduct, perfect livelihood, perfect effort, perfect mindfulness, perfect concentration.

'This Noble Truth of Suffering is a theory which was unknown to me before, and from which I derive my perception of this world, my clear-seeing, my wisdom, my knowledge, and my Awakening.

'Monks, you must surrender totally to this Noble Truth of Suffering. Monks, you must tear out the roots of suffering; I myself have done this. This Noble Truth must be spread abroad.

'Monks, as long as I lacked the perfect knowledge of these Four Noble Truths and their characteristics that form twelve subdivisions, I never pretended to men, to the gods, to the Maras, to the Brahmas, to the ascetics or the Brahmins, that I had attained to the supreme and perfect Awakening.'

'When I had acquired a right and proper knowledge
of the Four Noble Truths and their three characteristics
which, taken together, form twelve subdivisions, then I
began to teach the worlds of men and gods – as well as the
Maras, Brahmas, ascetics and Brahmins – that I had
attained to the supreme and perfect Awakening. Once more
I derived from this the knowledge and proper perception of
the world, so that my mind was perfectly emancipated, and
this is my last rebirth. I shall not be born again.'

After they had all heard these words, the Venerable
Kondann understood clearly that everything which is
susceptible to birth is also destined to die.

Then, as the Blessed One set in motion the Wheel
of the Teaching, the gods of the earth, according to myth,
began to shout:

'See, in the Deer Park at Isipatana near Varanasi, the
Blessed One has set in motion the Wheel of the Teaching,
which no ascetic can stop, nor a Brahma, nor a god, nor a
Mara nor a Brahmin.'

Hearing the sound of the Wheel, the gods of the
seven heavens and the Brahmas applauded. So, for a few

moments, cries of joy rose right up to the world of the
Brahmas and the ten thousand universes resonated and
echoed and trembled. An infinite and dazzling light shone
out across every universe, eclipsing the radiance of the gods.

Such is the jubilant account of legend.

In his joy, the Blessed One exclaimed: 'The Venerable
Kondann has mastered Truth; he is the victor.'
Henceforth, the Venerable Kondann was known
under the name of Anna Kondanna ('he who has made
himself master of the Truth'). The Venerable Kondanna
had totally embraced the Truth, leaving no room for
doubts. Victorious, he put his full trust in the Master's
teaching. 'Venerable Master', he cried, 'may I become a
monk with your blessing and receive ordination?' 'Come
hither, monk', answered the Buddha. 'Truth is expressed in
its proper form. Lead a noble life for the perfect cessation
of suffering.'
And so it was that Kondanna received ordination.
Then the Blessed One preached the Word and
lavished his counsel on the other monks. When they heard
the Buddha's advice and teaching, the Venerable Vappa

and the Venerable Bhaddiya clearly perceived the Truth; that everything which is susceptible to birth is also doomed to death. Like the Venerable Kondanna, they asked to receive ordination with the blessing of the Buddha.

All six shared the food which Kondanna, Bhaddiya and Vappa had collected as alms. The Venerable Mahanama and the Venerable Assaji then had a clear-sighted and perfect vision of the Truth, and asked to become monks. Their request was granted. Afterwards, the Blessed One turned to the five monks and said: 'In your opinion, is the body permanent or impermanent?' 'It is impermanent', was the reply. 'If something is impermanent, linked to suffering and liable to change, is it right to say: "Here is what I am, this is the real me?"' asked the Buddha. And the five monks answered: 'No, that cannot be.'

Similarly, the Buddha questioned them on sensations, perception, actions and consciousness, and they replied correctly.

Then the Buddha explained:

'Therefore, the body and its matter, whether in the present, the past, or the future, internally or externally, coarse or tender, pleasing or ugly, must be treated with

proper wisdom, and we must say of it: "This is not me."
The same is true of sensations, of perception, of actions
and consciousness.

'The noble disciple who sees things in this way will
not be attached to the body, to sensations, perceptions,
actions or consciousness. Then he will become detached.
And, through his detachment, he will become free. He will
have understood that he has become free and that he has
lived a noble life, that he has done what ought to have
been done and that there is nothing more to wish for.'

The five monks rejoiced at the words of the Buddha
and cast off all their bonds. So now there were six sages in
the world.

'There are, monks, gross impurities in gold: earth
or sand, gravel and grains of rock. So the goldsmith or his
apprentice first of all pours the gold into a trough and
washes it, rinses it, and dries it carefully.

'After the work of cleaning is done, some impurities,
not great yet not small, remain, such as sand and little
grains of rock. So the goldsmith or his apprentice washes
it, rinses it and dries it again.

'This done, there still remain tiny impurities like fine
sand or black dust. Then the goldsmith or his apprentice

renews his task, and it is only after all this that pure gold dust remains.

'He pours the gold into a crucible and heats it, stirring it till it melts. But he does not remove it from the vessel till all the impurities have disappeared, for the gold is as yet not malleable, not ready to be incised and not pure. It is still too hard and cannot be easily worked.

'But the moment comes when the imperfections begin to vanish, for the goldsmith and his apprentice have melted it again. Now the gold is malleable and ready to be moulded and shining bright. Whatever ornament the goldsmith wishes to make – be it a crown, earrings, a necklace or a chain – the gold is now ready to be moulded for this purpose.

'The same is true of a monk who strives for single-pointed concentration. There are gross impurities in this monk. He acts blindly, speaks blindly, thinks blindly. So the monk must reject these impurities and cast them out.

'Delivered from these, the mind of the monk, devoted to single-pointed concentration, still remains sullied by some degree of fault – blemishes that result from the desires of the senses, ideas of wickedness or of violence. Such thoughts the monk must reject.

'Yet even so, there remain subtle impurities in the mind of the monk who strives for single-pointed concentration: thoughts of his family, his country, his reputation.

'Having eliminated these, there remain only thoughts concerning higher states of the mind.

'This concentration is still not serene or purified. It has still not attained full peace of mind or absolute single-pointedness. It is not as yet unblemished.

'However, there comes a moment of inner strength; the mind becomes firm, unified, completely and utterly single-pointed. Then concentration is serene and purified; it knows perfect peace and unity.

'Finally, there may be states of mind accessible to superior wisdom – the wisdom for which we strive. But none may be reached save by superior thought and perception. Yet if the conditions are perfect, this shall come to pass.'

The Buddha had acquired his first disciples, the first of an endless series.

VULTURE PEAK

Rajgir~*Rajagrha*

Leaving Isipatana and Varanasi, the Buddha and his first disciples returned to the scene of his Awakening. They settled near Rajagrha in Magadha, the territory of King Bimbisara, on the hill known as Vulture Peak, some distance from the town.

The road leading up to the peak is steep and winding and allows the eye to take in a landscape composed of hills which appear as islands of green in the vast Plain of Bihar. The spot where the Buddha lived consists of huge blocks of rock which have cracked open to form little caves. The monks also built a few huts from branches to give themselves shelter. At present, on the slightly higher hill to the left and facing east, a Japanese Buddhist sect has built a temple linked to the town by a chairlift. All day long, from sunrise to sunset, the sound of an enormous drum booms out from the centre of the temple. A handful of Japanese monks are in residence; they receive visitors, who are especially numerous on festival days. A vast gilt statue of the Buddha, adjoining a white *stupa*, stares out towards Vulture Peak.

King Bimbisara, won over by the Buddha's philosophy and personality, presented him with the Bamboo Park and its lake. This place still exists; the park is well maintained, and there are also the remains of the foundations of the royal palace and other ruins such as the *stupa* where the ashes of Mahakashyapa were interred, the disciple who succeeded the Awakened One, and was converted here. (Compare the episode of the flower which the Buddha slowly turned between his fingers. Of all those present, only Mahakashyapa understood, and smiled. The Buddha, therefore, made him his successor and entrusted him with responsibility for the *sangha* or community of monks.) In another group of hills, further off, you can see the cave where, after the Master's death, the first council was held and the basic rules of teaching laid down. Rajagrha was the scene of numerous important events and encounters including the conversion of two other senior disciples, Sariputra and Maudgakyayana. It also witnessed an attempt on the life of the Blessed One, who, according to legend, was slightly injured by a boulder rolled down the hill by his own cousin, Devadatta, who was jealous of his influence.

We should add that, after the Buddha's arrival at Rajagrha, the order of events becomes somewhat confused. Though we know roughly where he spent the rainy seasons, it is difficult to assign accurate dates to events since he passed through the same places so many times. The *sutras* which relate the stories simply say: 'At that time the Blessed One was living in such-and-such a place.' But let us continue our journey as we began; stopping off here and there, we will choose an important event connected with each place to throw light on some aspect of the Buddha's mission.

For our stay at Rajgir, then, let's consider two encounters. One was with an assembly of prominent citizens, the other with someone he met on the way. In the first extract from the sacred texts, legend appears to have overtaken reality:

When the King of Magadha, Bimbisara, had instructed the elders of the villages in the laws of the visible world, he dismissed them. 'Friends,' he said, 'you have been instructed by me in the laws of the visible world; now go and approach the Blessed One. He will teach you the things of the other world.'

So the elders betook themselves to Mount Gijihakouta, which is the Peak of the Vultures. At this time, the duty of serving the Blessed One fell to the Venerable Sagata. They came to the Venerable Sagata, saying: 'We – the elders of the villages – are come to see the Blessed One. We ask you, Lord, to grant us the pleasure of his sight.' 'Wait here a while,' replied Sagata, 'and I will tell him you are come'.

Then the Venerable Sagata, who was standing at the top of the steps before the monastery, disappeared from the sight of the elders and entered the cell of the Blessed One. 'The elders of the villages are here to see the Blessed One,' said the Venerable Sagata. 'Do as you think fit, Lord.' 'Prepare me a seat, then, in the shade,' said the Blessed One. 'As you wish, Lord,' replied Sagata, leaving the presence of the Blessed One and returning to the top of the steps in the sight of the elders.

Then the Blessed One left his cell and came to sit on the seat prepared for him in the shade. The elders of the villages approached his seat; having prostrated themselves, they went and sat before the Blessed One. All of them, as it happened, turned their attention upon the Venerable Sagata, ignoring the Blessed One. The Blessed One divined at once what they were thinking and said to Sagata: 'Sagata, show them some miraculous thing; something which exceeds the power of man.' 'So be it, Lord,' replied the Venerable Sagata. Thereupon he levitated in the air. High up above them, he walked, stood upright, sat, lay down, breathed forth smoke and flames, and vanished. Having performed these various feats, Sagata then prostrated himself before the Blessed One. 'My lords,' he said to the elders, 'it is my Master who is the Blessed One; I am his disciple. I say to you again, my lords, my Master is the Blessed One; I am his disciple.'

Then the village elders thought: 'This is wonderful! This is a mighty thing indeed! If the disciple has such powers, what must the Master be!' They then turned their attention to the Blessed One, ignoring the Venerable Sagata. The Master proceeded to preach the Word to them, all things in due order: the sermon on alms, the sermon on

*righteousness, the sermon on heaven, on perversity, on
vanity, the stain of lust, on the glory of escaping the bonds
of passion. When he felt sure that their minds were
prepared, open, unfettered, uplifted and turned towards his
teaching, he preached them the sermon which belongs
above all to the Buddhas: on suffering, the origin of
suffering, the cessation of suffering, and the Way leading to
that cessation. Just as a piece of cloth that is without stain
will wholly receive the colour of a dye, so the elders, as they
sat there, felt a vision of the pure and unblemished Truth
arise within them: 'All things which may come to birth are
also destined to die.' Now they knew the doctrine and were
filled with its power. Possessing it, they abased themselves
before it, overcoming all doubts, laying aside all hesitation,
taking to their hearts this revelation; nor did they require
further instruction to perfect their belief in the doctrine of
the Master. Then they cried out to the Blessed One:
'Wondrous indeed are you, Lord! Just as a man rebuilds
what has been cast down, as a man brings to the light
what has been hidden; as in the darkness he lights a torch
that whoever has eyes may see what is before him; so the
Blessed One in many speeches has preached the doctrine.
Our trust, Lord, we place in the Blessed One and in the*

doctrine and in the community. Let the Blessed One be willing to receive us as his lay disciples, seeing that till the ending of our days we have placed our trust in him.'

The meeting with young Sigala, on the other hand, produced no miracles, though it turned out to be a moral lesson on how to live one's life.

Sigala was the son of a Buddhist family living near Rajagrha. He was completely indifferent towards religion, and his parents could not persuade him to go with them to visit the Buddha or his disciples and hear the noble doctrine. He thought it quite pointless, in fact, to have anything to do with the sangha – it would only entail material loss. He was only interested in profit and wealth, and therefore spiritual advancement made no sense to him. He said to his father:

'What have I to do with monks? Kneeling and prostrating myself will hurt my knees, and it will hurt my back. Then it would be necessary to sit upon the ground and dirty my clothes. And having talked with them of endless things which have no meaning at all, I would have to give them money or food. No, truly, I would be wasting

my time with such men.'

One day, however, the father fell ill and realized that his last hours had come. He called his son to his bedside and said: 'Son, do you respect these my last words?'

'Assuredly, O my father,' was the son's reply. 'I will respect your words, and do your bidding without delay.'

'In that case, my son, every morning, after your bath, you must greet the six regions: that is to say, the east, the west, the south, the north, the nadir and the zenith.'

The father had asked his son to do this, hoping that the Buddha or one of his disciples would one day notice him, talk to him, and maybe give him some useful information about the Way. So, after the old man's death, Sigala, respecting his father's last wishes, performed his greetings every morning, without the slightest idea of what they meant.

The Buddha had made a habit of finishing his sleep about four o'clock in the morning. He would then get up and sit in meditation for an hour. Afterwards, he went for a walk in the town or through the countryside and the villages to meet the people, to learn about their sufferings and bring them words of comfort. He always took his alms-bowl with him; people offered him a little food so he could

pass the day in the open when he chose. One morning,
after his meditation, he went to Rajagrha along a route
which passed close to Sigala's house. There he spotted the
boy, his body and hair still dripping wet; with hands joined,
he was greeting the six regions. Allowing him to finish, the
Buddha then asked him: 'Why are you doing this, young
farmer?' The young man answered:

'Lord, before he died, my father said to me: "Do
this". I am respecting his last wishes. Every morning I get
up early; after my bath, and before I leave for work, I greet
the six fundamental regions of the universe.'

'But, Sigala,' said the Buddha, 'there is yet another
way of respecting the six fundamental regions of the
universe. Yes, young farmer; he who has separated himself
from the four vices, who no longer sins through the four
evils, who does not waste his strength through the six
channels, who avoids these fourteen evil voices – he
respects the six fundamental regions of the universe, and
sets his foot upon the road which leads to victory in every
world. For he is the favourite son of this world of pomp
and show, and the favourite son of the world that is
beyond. And, after his body decays in death, his actions
continue in felicity.

'What then are the four vices from which a man must separate himself? Young farmer, they are: first, the destruction of life, then theft, then lewd sexual conduct, and finally untruth. These are the four vices to avoid.

'And what are the four ways of avoiding an evil action? Young farmer, when a man is led by desire, he commits evil. When he is led by anger, he commits evil. Led by ignorance, he also commits evil; led by fear, again he does evil.

'But if a man follows neither desire, nor anger, nor ignorance nor fear, he commits no evil action, for he does not transgress against the natural Way.

'Now what are the six channels which lead to the squandering of strength, power and riches?

'Indulgence in intoxicating liquors and drugs which enslave a man and take away his wits. Wandering the streets at foolish hours. The frequent attendance of shows and spectacles. The habit of gambling. Associating with evil companions. The habit of slothfulness.

'And, young farmer, there exist six evil consequences which attach themselves to the use of intoxicating liquors and drugs. A man loses his strength. More and more, he quarrels and fights. He is unable to resist sickness. He acquires an evil reputation. He loses his shame. His mind becomes weak.

'And, young farmer, there are six evil consequences awaiting whoever wanders in the streets late at night. That man is in great danger. His wife and children are in danger. Our goods and our houses are in danger. Such a man is suspected of evil intentions. Such a man is subject to false and lying rumours. Such a man will encounter a host of troubles.

'And, young farmer, there are six evil consequences awaiting the man who constantly frequents shows and spectacles, who is continually thinking: "Where may I go to dance? Where is there singing? Where can I go to hear music? Is there a play tonight? Is there an orchestra tonight? Where is a feast, where they smoke and drink?"

'And there are, young farmer, six evil consequences arising from involvement with gambling. When a man wins, he arouses hatred and envy. When he loses, he regrets what he has lost. He wastes his strength and his energy. His word is no longer believed. His friends and companions mistrust him. Women have no confidence in him, and all men say that a gambling man makes a bad husband.

'Young farmer, there are also six evil consequences which arise from association with companions who live unwholesome lives – those who gamble, those who give themselves up to pleasure, the drunkards and the gossips, the criminals and the violent men. Why? Because you will become just as they are.

'And again, young farmer, there are six evil consequences associated with slothfulness. A man decides he will not work because it is too cold, or it is too hot, or it is too late, or it is too early, or he is hungry, or he has eaten too much.

'Living in such a way, all his work is left unfinished, he cannot acquire new goods or possessions, and that which he has is spoiled.

'Drinking companions,' the Buddha added, 'are friends only when they are with you. Your companions are companions only so long as it suits them. Those who sleep until the going down of the sun, after they have slept till it has risen; those who take delight in sexual extravagances, who love nothing better than to drink, dance and make love to women every night; all those who continue to drink when they have already taken sufficient, who frequent the taverns, fall into debt as a stone tumbles into the water

and quarrel with their families; those licentious ones who
cannot maintain their homes, those who leave their work
unfinished and go about with wastrels; all these have
missed their chances, and they wane as the moon in
heaven wanes. They shall see their ruin.

'Furthermore, young farmer, beware of men who
flatter you, who demand much and offer little, who become
your companions for their own advantage, who make
agreeable propositions, who prattle of the past and the
future and try to win your favour with empty words; who,
when you require a service, prove themselves unable to
render it. Beware also of those who encourage your leanings
to evil, who disapprove of your desire to be charitable, who
praise you in your presence and malign you in your
absence. Do not associate with them, nor with those who
are absent ceaselessly from their house, nor those who seek
nothing but gambling and pleasure. A true friend, you will
discover, is constant, in evil times as in good; he is of good
counsel; he will offer you a refuge in danger, and supply
you in your need. A true friend will reveal his secrets and
confide them to your ears, does not forget you in
misfortune, tells you what you do not know, leads you in
the path of righteousness. Such a man will defend you

*before others, praise you in front of others; he will share
with you in your prosperity, and aid you in your misfortune.*

*'But surely, young farmer, you are wondering what
all this has to do with the six regions of the universe which
you must greet each morning. Well, then, I will tell you.
Your parents you must consider as the east, your teachers
as the south, your wife and your children as the west, your
friends and companions as the north, your servants and
workmen as the nadir, and finally, the ascetics and
Brahmins as the zenith.*

*'Whosoever is wise and virtuous, gentle, humble and
full of agreeableness, he shall know honour.*

*'Whosoever is busy and not slothful, who keeps
himself from misfortune, whose ways are adaptable and
intelligent, he shall know honour.*

*'Whosoever is hospitable and shows friendship, who
is liberal and open with others, who is as a guide, a
teacher, a counsellor, he shall know honour.*

*'Be generous, soft and quiet of speech, full of
compassion towards others and impartial toward all,
uttering words well-chosen for every occasion. These are
qualities as rare as any I have mentioned. And yet, these
qualities make the world go round, and are as needful to*

its proper progress as is the axle to the wheel of a cart.
If they did not exist, no mother or father would receive the
respect of their children. If these qualities exist, then
wisdom may arise in any place.'

When the Buddha had finished, the young farmer
exclaimed:

'Thank you, Lord, thank you with all my heart! You
have straightened in me what was crooked, you have
revealed in me what was hidden, you have shown me the
Way when I was lost, you have enlightened me in my
darkness, you have made my eyes which were blind to see
again. This you have done by instructing me in all these
things. Thank you, Lord, thank you with all my heart!
Consider me henceforth as one of your disciples.'

The Buddha smiled, and nodded gently. Leaning on
his staff, his alms-bowl still in his other hand, he slowly
continued on his way to the village of Rajagrha. The sun
had now risen above the wooded hills and its rays were
searching out the deepest nooks in the valleys. 'It will be
hot today,' he thought.

The Practice of Meditation

Let's return for the moment to the subject of meditation. Indeed, the sermons and homilies forming the core of the *sutras* were themselves based on the assiduous practice of a ritual involving sitting in a state of tranquil concentration. All disciples – both monks and nuns – were required to perform this daily, and sometimes, during retreats, several times a day. Here, for instance, is the exercise involving concentration upon the process of breathing:

> *'A monk who dwells in the forest, or who dwells at the foot of a tree, or who dwells in an empty room, sits down cross-legged, his back erect, his face bearing the signs of*

vigilant thought. His mind is bent upon his breathing in and
his breathing out. When he breathes in a long breath, he
thinks, "I am breathing in a long breath." When he breathes
out a long breath, he thinks, "I am breathing out a long
breath." When he breathes in a short breath, he thinks, "I
am breathing in a short breath." And so on, monks.'

The Buddha states that this exercise – an excellent
one and full of joy – releases the evil which wells up inside
us. When the disciples were asked how their Master was
accustomed to spend the season of the rains, they had to
reply:

'Seated in deep concentration on his breathing in and
his breathing out. Thus, O my friends, the Blessed One is
accustomed to remain during the season of the rains.'

The Buddha himself, then, continued to practise the
meditation which formed the basis of his Awakening for the
rest of his life. He explains:

'Having sought alms and eaten my meal, I go away
into the forest. I make a pile with the grass and leaves

which I find there. I sit down upon the pile, with my legs crossed, my back erect, and compose my face into the attitude of vigilant thought. Thus I remain, allowing the force of my well-wishing, which my thoughts are full of, to pour out upon one of the quarters of the world. And likewise upon the second, the third, the fourth, upwards, downwards, horizontally. In all directions and in all its fullness, upon the entirety of the universe, I allow the force of my loving-kindness, of which my thoughts are full, to pour forth around me, vast, immeasurable, inexhaustible, knowing no hatred, pursuing no hurtfulness.'

The root of his teaching is as follows:

Just as he who includes in his thoughts the vastness of the ocean must necessarily include all the streams which flow into the ocean; likewise, whoever develops the attentive contemplation of the body through frequent meditation will also attain all those states which are part of the supreme wisdom. One thing leads to the awakening of awareness, to a great good, to a great freedom from destiny, to the fullness of being and to understanding, to the acquiring of proper vision and knowledge, to the prize

*of deliverance. This thing, monks, if it is practised and
developed with diligence, consists of the attentive
contemplation of the body through the practice of
meditation. By this practice alone, the body is calmed, the
mind likewise; useless thoughts give place to thoughts of
wisdom, which are brought to their fullness and
completion. By a single practice assiduously developed,
ignorance is cast aside, wisdom is born, delusions
concerning self disappear and the chains of sense-awareness
are broken. This single practice is the attentive
contemplation of the body ... Those who have not acquired
it cannot partake of the immortal mind; they are
unmindful of non-death, non-death is not comprehended
by such persons.*

*'Through this practice, a person may conquer
himself. But if a person is overcome by cravings and desire
– contemptible things and fiercely rooted in this world –
the sorrows of this man shall flourish as the grass
flourishes in the field. But whosoever overcomes these
desires, these contemptible cravings, from which in this
world it is a hard thing to escape, his sorrow shall fall
away as a drop of water falls from the petal of the lotus.*

'Just as, if the root of a tree is intact, and it is cut

down, the tree will grow again with great vigour; so, if the causes of desire are not slain, sorrow continually uprises to pierce the heart of a man.

'Greater than all things present is the present nature of Truth. Greater than all loving-kindness is the loving-kindness of Truth. Greater than all joy is the joy that dwells in Truth. With the cessation of desire ceases all pain.'

And the pain is that existential angst which we need to conquer inside of us:

'When a lay person, to whom the Way is not known, experiences pain, he is unhappy and afflicted; he laments and beats his breast and wrings his hands, he weeps and his spirit melts away. Thus it is said that this person has not emerged from the bottomless abyss. But when a noble disciple, who has received the teaching, experiences pain, he is neither unhappy nor afflicted, he does not lament nor does he need to wring his hands and weep, nor does his spirit melt away. Thus it is said that the noble disciple has emerged from the bottomless abyss and has stood upon the ground with firm feet.

'Why? Because he has obtained mastery of his mind

and knows that pain is but the result of actions and karma
belonging to the past. Therefore he will control this pain.'

This also allows him to conquer the fear of death, as
we see from this story:

*Sariputra and Upacena were living at that time near
Rajagrha in a cave known as the 'Serpents' Cavern'. One
day, a serpent struck the Venerable Upacena. He turned to
the monks and said: 'Friends, take away this body, put it
on a litter and carry it outside, for soon it will be dispersed
like a handful of straw.'*

*To which Sariputra replied: 'Venerable monk, we see
no change in your body, no change in your faculties.'*

*'It is true, Sariputra my friend, that for he who
thinks "I am the eye, the eye is part of me", or "I am the
ear, the ear is part of me", or "I am the nose, the nose is
part of me", or "I am the tongue, the tongue is part of
me", or "I am the body, the body is part of me", or "I am
the mind, the mind is part of me", for him, indeed, the
onset of death can be a moment of terror, which alters his
body and his faculties. But in my case, my friend, since I do
not think that I am the eye and that this eye is part of me,*

that I am the mind and this mind is part of me, there can be no alteration in my body, nor in my faculties.'

As they listened, the monks understood that the Venerable Upacena was announcing his death as a saint was expected to. So they placed his body on a litter and carried it outside.

Little by little, the life of the Venerable Upacena was dispersed like a handful of straw. For five things are impossible in this world: to stop ageing once we have started, not to be ill when we are ill, to prevent ourselves from dying when the moment arrives, to halt the dispersal of the matter forming our bodies, and to stop the extinction of life that is ending. Every human being in the world is faced by these necessities, and yet, if he has understood the Buddha's message, he will not suffer, for he accepts their inevitability. In the universal future, there is no distinction between the process of life and that of decay, just as in the heights of heaven there is neither east nor west nor south nor north. It is only humanity which makes such distinctions, and places birth at the opposite extreme to death. But to the mind of a Buddha, the world is no more than a passing cloud.

ACTIONS AND THE ACTOR

Nalanda

A few miles from Rajgir is Nalanda with its *stupa* dedicated to Sariputra, the theologian of the Buddha's *sangha*, who was born and died here. Around the *stupa* are scattered the impressive ruins of a monastery, and a Buddhist university, founded in all probability by the Gupta emperors in the fifth and sixth centuries CE. This university was renowned throughout Asia; the famous Chinese pilgrim, Hsuan Tsang, declared that it contained several thousand monks studying not only the Mahayana and the Theravada, but also logic, medicine, and purely Brahmin texts such as the *Vedas*. The regime was strict and the place was buzzing from morning to night with erudite discussion. But the school fell upon hard times with the decline of Buddhism in India, and was also to come under attack by Muslims in the thirteenth century.

The first archaeological digs began in 1915. It has to be said that the university at Nalanda, whatever the beauty of its site, proved to be one of the reasons for the decline of Buddhism. In fact, the monks based there sank deeper and deeper into more and more abstruse discussions, neglecting the basic practices of meditation and intellectualizing this approach to self-discovery to an impossible degree. This created an elitist philosophy, divorced from the real world and real people. On the other hand, all the great Masters of Buddhism – those of Theravada, Ch'an, Zen, who were responsible for its expansion – adopted an essentially practical approach, basing their teaching, however learned, on the fundamental techniques advocated by the Buddha and reviving his quintessential perceptions of the nature of reality and everyday experience.

This did not prevent the Buddha from arguing with proponents of alternative theories and engaging in now-famous dialectical battles, which contributed to the development of what he termed his creative work: the *dharma* or teaching:

'My work is my wealth, my work is my heritage, my work is the breast which suckles me. My work is the family to which I belong, my work is all that I have.'

The Buddha insisted on the fact that the doer – or actor – was of secondary importance to the deed – or action. All individuality, he stated, is composed of the sum total of the individual's past actions and his actions evolving in the present; this total constitutes a coherent flux of energy which we define as that person or individual. The following anecdote will shed new light on this philosophical theory, the implications of which have much in common with the advanced scientific hypotheses of today.

The Buddha was living at the time in Nalanda in a monastery. It had been built amidst a splendid park of mango trees by a benefactor named Pavarika, a rich merchant. During the same period, Mahavira, the spiritual leader of the Jain sect, was also living in the town with a whole troupe of ascetic disciples who went about naked. One of them, Tapassi, came to see the Buddha, who offered him a low seat beside him.

'Well now, Tapassi,' said the Buddha, 'your master

Mahavira – how many types of actions does he say are the
result of evil desires?'

'Venerable Gautama, he does not use the word
action; he calls it aggression. He says that there exists the
aggression created by the body, that created by words, and
that created by the mind.'

'And which of these types of aggression proves the
most dangerous when a man feels evil desires and brings
them to pass?'

'Mahavira says that hostile states of the body,
aroused by evil, are the most dangerous.'

And three times the Buddha made the naked ascetic
confirm that the body is responsible for the worst forms
of aggression. Tapassi then asked him what was his own
opinion on the matter.

'First of all, Tapassi,' answered the Buddha, 'in my
teaching I do not use the words aggression or hostility, but
the word action. There are in fact three types of actions
arising from evil. Those created by the body, by words, and
by the mind. But of these three different types, I consider
mental actions as the most dangerous and the most
poisonous; yes, the actions of the mind are the most full
of hatred.'

'So mental actions – those created by the mind – are the worst, Venerable Gautama?'

The naked ascetic made Gautama confirm this three times before leaving his seat and going to rejoin his master, Mahavira. The latter, who was sitting under the shade of a tree surrounded by a tribe of villagers led by a certain Upali – the local lord – saw his naked disciple returning.

'Where have you come from like that? Where have you been in the heat of the midday sun?' he called out.

'Master,' replied Tapassi,' I have been to see the Venerable Gautama to talk with him'. And he related what had passed between them.

'You have done very well,' said Mahavira, 'you have explained our doctrine clearly. For what is the hostility of the mind and the word, compared with that arising from the body? The aggression of the mind is as nothing compared with the aggression of the body!'

Then their host, Upali, turned to Mahavira:

'How clear your doctrine is! I shall go and see this Gautama; if he continues to preach this false doctrine, I will compel him by force to debate with me, that I may show him how wrong he is. As a ploughman falls upon his land with the plough, as a wrestler seizes his opponent around his body, as an elephant charges his rival, I will go and confront Gautama.'

'Go and do this then,' replied Mahavira.

But Tapassi, the naked ascetic, intervened.

'Master,' he said, 'you are wrong to send him like this. The Venerable Gautama is a magician. If he meets the disciple of another religion, he will bewitch him.'

'That is impossible, Tapassi. The truth is quite otherwise. It is probably our friend, Upali, with his strength and his force, who will convince Gautama and make him his disciple instead. One of us must refute the error that Gautama has been putting about. Leave this matter to our host, Tapassi.'

So Upali got up, bowed to Mahavira and the crowd of people, and went off to the park of mango trees where the Buddha was living. The latter offered him a seat beside him. Upali then asked what exactly had passed between him and Tapassi, the naked ascetic. Once he had his answer, Upali exclaimed:

'The naked ascetic has clearly shown you that in the matter of evil, the hostility of the mind has little importance compared with that of body. Only the body can do real harm; the aggression of the mind and the aggression of words are, in the end, of little consequence.'

'Upali,' answered the Buddha, 'if you yourself wish to learn the Truth, if you wish to argue with me, then let us debate together.'

'Yes, let us debate on this subject.'

'Suppose, Upali, that there is a naked ascetic who observes the four prohibitions. He does not kill, nor encourage killing, nor consent to killing. He does not steal, nor encourage stealing, nor consent to stealing. He does not lie, nor encourage lying, nor consent to lying. He does not abandon himself to the pleasures of the senses, he does not encourage these pleasures, nor does he condone them. And yet, every day, this man – who has distanced himself from evil – kills little creatures by treading upon them or eating them; thus he scatters death and destruction about him. What does Master Mahavira say then of such a thing?'

'Venerable One, Mahavira declares that an action which is not intentional cannot be evil or harmful.'

'But if the action is intentional, will it be harmful?'

'Of course.'

'Then how does Mahavira define this intentional action?'

'He defines it as an aggression of the mind.'

'O Upali, Upali, take care and think before you answer, for you have just contradicted your own doctrine.'

'But, Gautama, that does not prevent the hostility created by the body from being more harmful than that created by the mind.'

'Well, then, let us suppose that a warrior arrives and decides to destroy this town of Nalanda using only his physical strength and his sword. Will he accomplish this destruction?'

'No, for soon fifty men will come against him. What can he do against fifty, all alone?'

'Good. Suppose now that a Brahmin, whose mental powers are superior, who has mastery of men's minds, suppose that he decides to impose his will upon this town by the power of his mind and his hatred? Will he accomplish this?'

'He could reduce ten, twenty, thirty, forty and even more towns by the force of his hatred and his will! He could crush the spirit of the people under his yoke and make himself their master!'

'Well then, Upali, that hardly seems to prove your argument! Which, then, is the stronger action, that of the mind or that of the body?'

'Venerable Gautama, you have convinced me; moreover, as soon as I saw you, I knew you were right. The power of the mind is superior in evil-doing to the power of the body, which is no more than its tool. If the mind is full of hate, the body is its slave. I would therefore like to become your disciple.'

'Do not abandon your old beliefs after one conversation!'

'Venerable One, any holy man would be proud of my decision and would proclaim it to the world. But you, you are rejecting me. I wish to become your disciple and take refuge in the light of your instruction.'

'If you so wish, Upali. But do not forget – until today, you have taken in and fed the naked ascetics. You must continue to help those who pass by seeking alms, whatever their beliefs.'

'Venerable One, I thought you would answer like the others, saying "Your alms must be given to my disciples alone", but you bid me leave my house open and feed the naked ascetics when they ask me. Lord, for the third time, I prostrate myself as your disciple and wish to share your compassion.'

The Upali Sutra goes on to tell how the Buddha, seeing that this man's mind was ready, open, lucid and uplifted, revealed to him little by little the Truth concerning the Way which leads to the cessation of suffering. It also tells us that when he returned home after thanking the Buddha, Upali ordered his gate-keeper to close his gates in future to naked ascetics, male or female, but to give them food if they asked for it – outside. On the other hand, he told him to open the gates to the disciples of the Buddha wearing their robes. This quickly became known in the region and Mahavira, the leader of the Jains, decided to come and see for himself, with a horde of naked ascetics, what Upali was doing:

The gate-keeper came to the gates and refused to let them in, relaying his master's orders and offering them food if they were hungry. Furious, Mahavira commanded him to go and tell Upali he was there and wished to see him. This was done; the host prepared seats and received the band of naked ascetics in the central entrance hall. However, he did not go to meet them, and waited for them on the highest seat.

'Are you stupid or crazy?' shouted Mahavira. 'The other day you went away to refute the Lord Gautama, but

now you have come back entwined in the snares of debate.
You have emasculated yourself, you have cast yourself into
a net made of words, you have been caught up by deceit
as a man who is baffled by a magician's trick.'

'Ah, Lord! If all the members of my family and all
my friends and relations could fall under this spell you are
talking of, that would quickly restore them to good sense
and happiness. If all the warlords, all the merchants, all the
Brahmins, all the ordinary people and all the powers and
divinities could be bewitched by that magic, their
deliverance would be at hand. But let me tell you a story.

'An old Brahmin had married a young wife and
made her with child. One day, this woman asked him to
go to the market and look for a young monkey to play with
her child when it was born. The old husband then asked
her, would she mind waiting till after the birth? He wished
to buy a male monkey for a boy, a female one for a girl.
But she insisted, and the Brahmin, bound by the chains of
love, carried out his promise. When he came back from the
market with the monkey, his wife said: "Go and take the
monkey to the dyer and ask him to dye the animal the
colour of gold inside and outside, then wring it out to dry
and iron it with hot irons to straighten out its coat." And

*the Brahmin, bound by the chains of love, did as she
asked. But the dyer said to him: "If you insist, your monkey
can be dyed on the outside; but if you wish to have it back
alive, it cannot be dyed on the inside, nor wrung out and
ironed with hot irons."*

'The same is true of your teaching, Mahavira. It may
convince and delight simple people, but certainly not those
with any sense. The teaching of the Buddha, on the other
hand, can be compared to the ending of this story. This
same Brahmin went back to the dyer with some old
clothes. And the dyer said: "Yes, to be sure, I can dye these
clothes gold on each side, then wring them out and iron
them immaculately." So it is with the doctrine of the
Buddha: it is simple and practical, made for those with
clear minds and not madmen, a doctrine that will stand
the test.'

*White with rage, Mahavira cried: 'Whose disciple are
you now then, Upali?'*

Upali rose and replied:

'I am the disciple of him who frees man from
ignorance, possesses wisdom and a right-thinking mind,
who has progressed beyond doubts.

'I am the disciple of him who is not perplexed,

whose spirit is all compassion, who has renounced vain pleasures, who was born as a man, but who bears his final incarnation.

'I am the disciple of him whose nature is pure, for he has broken the chains of delusions, pride, and the desire to be heroic.

'I am the disciple of him who has passed beyond all passions, has emancipated himself from obsessions and fantastical dreams.

'I am the disciple of him who is no hypocrite, whose being has embraced peace, who has ennobled his personality and developed his intuition.

'I am the disciple of him who is free from loving and hating, who has crossed the ocean of sorrow and wishes to show others how to cross.

'I am the disciple of him who is calm, confident, skilful and good; of him who cannot be swayed or influenced, for he has reached perfection; of him whose vision is clear for he has passed beyond "I" and "me"; of him who absorbs himself in proper meditation. Yes, of that man, blessed above all others, I have become the disciple.'

The *sutra* tells us that at these words Mahavira, in his

jealousy and rage, spat out a jet of blood as he left; he was only to meet the Buddha much later in life. Though Mahavira remained head of a sect which still has its adherents in India today, he would develop a deep admiration for the exceptional inner strength of the Buddha and the dignity of his bearing. He came to respect the Awakened One's teaching and, according to the chronicles, died before him.

The story of Mahavira, Upali and the Buddha is typical of the relations existing at the time between the Buddha and other sects. The more jealous and envious the latter became, the more the Awakened One replied to their attacks and criticisms with tolerance and detailed argument, striving to convince his opponents without trying to lure them away from their beliefs, hoping to dissipate the mists of error resulting from their confusion. His dialectic is skilful, deriving from his royal upbringing, from his experience of life, from his long and deep exploration of himself during his years of asceticism and from his regular practice of meditation. Throughout his life, this practice enabled him to maintain a state of awareness in which he could empathize with others but remain detached from the bonds of the mental and physical pain experienced by them.

The impression we receive is that, while he was very accessible, he also looked upon everything with a perspicacity which, admittedly, denotes a certain aloofness. And yet – this is the immense appeal of his message – he possessed the gift of showing others how to discover this insight and of enabling them to share it. This, of course, is what discovery and revelation is all about. He was not so much interested in convincing people and acquiring disciples, or in defending one theory of the universe as opposed to another, as he was in passing on his own experiences of a practice which, even within our own bodies, transcends the sum total of the waking state as it is habitually perceived. It was a matter of a different approach, of discovering a wider sense of experience and awareness, and then of enlarging its bounds ever further, till it encompassed the infinity of possibilities and characteristics existing in every individual. The essential task was the acquisition of clear-sightedness:

'Everything that a man is, is the fruit of the mind, has for its essence mind, is composed of the mind. If a man speaks or acts with an evil mind, then sorrow will follow him as the wheel follows the foot of the draught-ox.

Everything that we are is the fruit of the mind, has for its essence the mind, is composed of the mind. If a man speaks or acts with a pure mind, joy will follow like his shadow, which never leaves him.'

So it is reported in the *Dharmapada*.

Finally, we ought to state that the Buddha's message, this philosophy with its thorough seasoning of common sense, proved all the more influential in that he was known to practise what he preached:

'If a person utters many wise words but acts unwisely, he is a fool, and like a herdsman who counts the cows of another, he has no share in the dignity of the monks. But he who utters few wise words, but conducts himself according to the law of Truth, who abstains from love and hatred and blindness of spirit, who possesses wisdom, and whose mind has discovered deliverance, who is attached to nothing either on earth or in heaven ... he has a share in the dignity of the monks.'

Thus he succeeded in creating an active community,

each member of which was on the way to becoming a Buddha capable of awakening more Buddhas still. Buddhahood exists in everyone; it is a matter of discovering it. But we must not press this point – you can lead a horse to water, but you can't make it drink. Similarly, it is possible to show someone the Way, to give advice and instructions for the journey; but the actual walking must be done by that person alone. A solitary walker with a solid faith.

Parables

The Buddha also told many parables to his disciples. The stories played on the power of imagination and the association of ideas.

'I want to tell you a parable; it is thanks to parables that many a wise man discovers the meaning of what is said.'

The subject-matter of the parables was drawn equally from human behaviour and from the natural world; they dealt with spiritual life, the observance of proper practices, deliverance and the community. The Buddha's preaching on deliverance is comparable to the work of the doctor extracting a poisoned arrow from a wound and using medicinal plants to combat the poison.

The community of the disciples, this assembly of noble minds, amid which all worldly distinctions of rank disappear, is like the sea with all its wonders. In its depths lie pearls and precious stones; giant creatures toss about on its bosom; rivers pour into it, losing their names, for all are become part of the sea, every one, as many as there are. The labourer ploughs his field, sows his seeds, waters his crop, but he has not the power to say: 'Today the seed must germinate, tomorrow it must spring up, the next day it must ripen.' He must wait for the proper season for his crop to grow and mature. The same is true of the disciple striving to obtain deliverance. He must subject himself to austerity, devote himself to meditation, instruct himself ardently in the doctrine of salvation. But he has no power to say: 'Today or tomorrow, my mind must be set free.'

The Way is trodden step after step, moment after moment:

'Imagine, O disciples, a forest on the side of a

mountain. In the forest is a deep swamp and a pool, beside which lives a great tribe of wild beasts. And a man comes along intent upon destroying these beasts and sowing grief and destruction amongst them. He conceals the track by which one can pass easily and safely, and prepares a false track, a track leading into the swamp. Then, O disciples, the great tribe of wild beasts will henceforth suffer hurt and danger, and decrease. But, if now there comes a man intent upon the prosperity, the well-being and the happiness of that great tribe of savage beasts, this man will open up and clear the track by which one can pass easily and safely, destroy the false track, obliterate the path that leads to the swamp, the boggy path. And so the great tribe of wild beasts will henceforth prosper, increase and multiply. This parable I have told you to make you understand. Now the meaning is this: the great swamp and the pool, O disciples, are the pleasures. The great tribe of wild beasts, these are human beings. The man who plots evil, misfortune and suffering is Mara, the Evil One. The false path is the False Eightfold Path, which is: false view, false resolve, false speech, false conduct, false livelihood, false effort, false mindfulness, false concentration. The way to the swamp is indulgence and craving. The way to the swamp, O disciples, is ignorance.'

This evil spirit within us which is personified by Mara, the tempter, is a malevolent energy which is very real and must be hunted out with the greatest vigilance:

'Once upon a time there was a tortoise who went to the riverbank at dusk to search for food. And a jackal also came along to the river in the twilight looking for prey. When the tortoise saw the jackal, she hid herself entirely in her shell and remained very still and quiet. The jackal ran up and waited for her to put out her head or her tail or one of her legs. But she did not budge, and the jackal had no choice but to abandon his prey and go away.

'So, O disciples, Mara is watching you constantly, and he is always thinking: "By way of their eye I want to get inside them – or by way of their ear, of their nose, of their tongue, of their body, of their mind, I want to get inside them." That is why, O disciples, you must guard well the ways of your senses ... Then Mara, the Evil One, will give up and leave you alone, if he finds no way inside you, just as the jackal had to leave the tortoise.'

These were parables designed for simple minds – probably numerous among the Buddha's listeners. For others, whose intellect was more developed, his language,on the same subjects reveals that he had evolved a genuine theory of behavioural psychology which, if we update the terminology somewhat, can be explained as follows. If a lay person trains his mind to the ideal of purity, the knowledge he acquires will condition his behaviour to be pure. If he trains his mind with the opposite aim, his knowledge will condition impure behaviour. If he aims at neither quality, and is indifferent, likewise his behaviour will be conditioned by indifference. But take the case of a monk. If he has emancipated himself from ignorance and obtained Enlightenment, his behaviour is conditioned neither by purity nor impurity nor indifference ... That monk in fact fulfils his duty: to acquire a consciousness which is non-discriminatory, that is, perfectly universal. He has developed what advanced psychology calls bio-awareness.

Master Deshimaru explained this to us one day very clearly:

'When the "I", the ego, has disappeared, duality ceases. If there is "I" and "others", duality exists. When there is no more "I", there are no more "others". What we

have instead is interdependency. This we may call "non-thought."

'You must not limit your thoughts with words and phrases. If you make categories for yourself, then, from that moment, words are futile. Europeans always create categories with words and sometimes they run into contradictions. This is an inevitable weakness of language. I ask: "What is that?", "That is that," you say. But by saying "that" you are leaping to conclusions. "What is that?", "That is a kyosaku (a stick)." But it is also true to say: "That is wood." Again, "What is that?" "It is oak." This is true, too. In Zen, discussions are always like that. Someone says: "A flame moves." Another says: "No, it is not the flame moving, but the wind." Yet another, a cleverer person, says: "It is neither the wind nor the flame, but your mind that is moving." And, finally, someone else says: "It is neither the wind, nor the flame, nor your mind ..." You need to understand why others are not you. If I cannot do something, I cannot explain it. I am not others. I am what I am. I am myself. I do not need to follow others.

'There are many interpretations for the statements "I am what I am" and "I do not need to follow others." I must decide for myself. I must practise for myself. Others

are not me, it is true, yet your mind and mine possess the
same substance. I am like heaven, I am like the earth.
When a person abandons all, he becomes the other. It is
the abandonment of the ego. The end of delusion.'

The Buddha spoke about becoming the flux of cosmic energy:

'There is, O disciples, a dimension, where there is
neither land nor water nor air nor light, nor infinity of
space nor infinity of the reason, nor total absence of all
things, nor simultaneous suppression of representation and
non-representation, nor this world nor that, and at the
same time neither sun and nor moon. O disciples, I call it
neither coming nor going, nor remaining, nor death nor
birth. Without beginning, without change, without end. It
is the cessation of suffering.

There exists, O disciples, the unborn, the uncreated,
the unoriginated, the unconditioned. If there did not exist,
O disciples, the unborn, the uncreated, the unoriginated,
the unconditioned, there would be no escape from the
born, the created, the originated, the conditioned.'

This form of philosophy considers the absence of phenomena and the presence of phenomena as interdependent, a concept attested by present-day science, and described also in the works of philosophers such as Eckhart in the fourteenth century and Heidegger in the twentieth. There is no dichotomy between non-existence and existence.

CONSCIOUSNESS
AS ILLUSION

Ayodhya and Other Places

This sort of teaching, pitched at different levels, is dispensed wherever we travel through northern India, in the countryside and in villages and cities alike. This is certainly the case at Ayodhya, on the banks of the Ganges, one of the seven sacred cities of India, the territory of the monkey-god, Hanuman, and the yogis. Here, Buddhist theory has to grapple with other beliefs centring around religious devotion to particular deities.

Vibrant with sounds and chanting, its atmosphere laden with incense-smoke, Ayodhya is a city few Westerners visit. It has been held sacred since time immemorial; away from the tourist circuit, it is alive with religious fervour.

There are constant processions, frenetic parades of Hindhu pilgrims chanting their mantras and the name of Rama. Priests hand out garlands of flowers, gather up the small coins thrown to them and urge the throng of devotees to adore the images of the gods. These images are painted in garish colours, dressed in gold brocade, and put out on public display. In the streets, people are preparing huge piles of red and ochre powder for the ritual painting of the worshippers' faces. The marble paving-stones of the temples are cool and fresh underfoot. The atmosphere resembles the fervour of medieval times – fascinating and magical. Religion here is not merely a moral support but also the expression of people's hopes and dreams.

In an out-of-the way street are the living quarters of the *sadhus*, near a temple dedicated to Rama, where a famous guru dispenses his wisdom. This is an extraordinary place; it might just be some shady, run-down area of the city, were it not for the obvious cleanliness and dignity of these men who have chosen an itinerant life and voluntary poverty in their search for the path to heaven. Beside the temple are vast kitchens; some monks work naked in the heat of the sunken ovens, where chapattis are tossed into piles against the walls. In one corner of the temple, the guru, sitting with his back against a column, receives his visitors, who form a long queue. He is a huge, bearded man with an ironic and piercing gaze. Seeing us pass, he has us called over and asks the reason for our visit. Kneeling like the other pilgrims, we briefly explain our journey. He smiles, blesses us, hands us some sugar-candies. We bow, and he turns to somebody else. One of his followers shows us out into an enormous room resembling a half-built cathedral where a hundred or so *sadhus* – some extremely young – are chanting the name of Rama, in unison, to the accompaniment of a harmonium. As we approach, their chantings redouble in strength. Their faces are radiant, their voices are quivering with the emotion of their faith. A moment of great intensity.

As we leave, an old *sadhu* starts yelling at the top of his voice as soon as he spots us: 'Heretics, depart from the Holy City, for you profane it!' He is gently led away by other monks. This is the only time we encounter any show of intolerance.

But this was obviously an example of blind faith taken to the extreme: *bhakti-yoga*, the yoga of adoration and pure devotion.

In the centre of this city, where Buddha apparently

lived, we climb a spiral staircase to the top of a mound. Then our guide conducts us to a temple which has the reputation that prayers made to the goddess here are granted. Since I started to climb this hill, I have been feeling rather dizzy and a bit sick: probably due to tiredness from the journey, the stifling heat here, and maybe some virus or other.

We arrive at the temple, where it seems that all the famous figures in India have at some time come to appease the goddess; Indira Gandhi, for instance. We are astonished to find the place so dirty and dilapidated, tucked away in an inner suburb. While the goddess is being 'fed' behind a filthy curtain – believers bring the food, which the priests then tuck into a little later – a few peasant families in rags stand waiting on the threshold. I start to feel worse. The curtain opens, the statue of the goddess appears. She has a black face and is dressed in gold brocade; a whole cluster of earrings hangs from each of her ears. Beside her stand two very grim-looking priests who harangue the wretched peasants and remind them that the goddess answers every prayer. They look at the priests with the air of beaten dogs, bring out their pennies and small coins. Somewhat undecidedly, I turn and head for the way out. But, in the porch, I tell myself I might as well make a prayer, just for the sake of it. If Indira Ghandi did it, I can, too; it's now or never. I turn back, bow to the altar and proclaim that I want to feel better immediately.

In the car on the way to Lucknow, dozing in the back seat, my ears full of 'Rama, Rama, Rama, O Rama', I feel absolutely fine. (This was to be the last health worry during the trip.)

Psychosomatic?

Maybe, maybe not. But the fact remains that the Buddha found himself obliged to make enormous efforts to counter the old vision of things. Witness, for example, this fine sermon which he delivered one day to the monks:

'Monks, if a huge mass of foam were to float down the Ganges and an eagle-eyed man noticed it and went to examine it carefully, he would see that it was empty, without consistency and proper substance. For what indeed could be the substance of foam?

'Likewise, matter, including the body – past, future or present, internal or external, gross or subtle, high or low, near or far – if observed by a monk, would seem empty, without substance and consistency. For indeed, what

substance could matter have?

'If, in autumn, when the rains fall in heavy drops, a bubble came to the surface of the water and then disappeared, and an eagle-eyed man came along, saw it, and examined it closely, it would appear to him empty, without consistency or substance. For indeed, what could be the substance of a bubble on the water?

'The same ought to be true, monks, of every sensation or feeling – past, present or future – examined by a monk; it would appear to him as empty, without consistency or substance. For what substance could a sensation have?

'If, in the last month of the hot season, at midday, a mirage were to appear, and an eagle-eyed man were to see it and consider it, it would appear to him as empty, without consistency and substance. For what could be the substance of a mirage?

'Likewise, every perception examined by a monk would appear to him empty, without consistency and substance. For what substance could there be in perception and the activity of the mind which derives from it?

'Imagine that a magician or his assistant performs an illusion by the roadside and that an eagle-eyed man

comes along, sees it and considers it carefully. The thing would appear to him to be empty, without consistency or substance. For what substance could there be in an illusion?

'The same is true of consciousness. If a monk considers it in all its aspects, it would appear to him to be empty, without consistency or substance. For what substance could there be in consciousness?

'The noble disciple, perceiving the world in this manner, abandons all emotional links with body, sensations, perception, consciousness and the activities of the mind.

'Devoid of these, he becomes detached. Detached, he is delivered, and, in deliverance, exists the awareness of being delivered. And he knows that birth is over and done with, life is lived and ended. What ought to have been accomplished is accomplished. Nothing more remains of any state at all.'

The Blessed One then continued:

'The son of the sun has explained
How matter is comparable to the foam of the ocean,

Sensation to a bubble on the water,
Perception and memory to a mirage,
How consciousness is an illusion.
However a man may observe them,
Examine them with every care,
They reveal themselves empty and without substance
For him who views them with wisdom.

'This body – to which he teaches
Wisdom in its immensity –
Once deprived of these three things
Is abandoned and rejected:
Life, heat, consciousness.
When the body is deprived of these,
It lies there, abandoned,
Inanimate, mere food for other creatures;
This is the destiny of body –
A chattering illusion,
It is called destiny the slayer,
Empty of all substance.

'This is how a monk with great energy
Ought to consider all these entities,

Continually, day and night,
In the fullness of wisdom and mindfulness.

'Let him cast off all his chains,
Build his own safe refuge,
Go forth in quest of immortality
As if his spirit were on fire.'

And wherever he went, sermons, parables and dialogues followed one another.

Once, the Buddha passed the night in a forest; the forest of simsapa *trees in the region of Alavi. He had slept on a bed of leaves, which he had spread on the ground. In the morning, the son of the King of Alavi, Hatthaka, happened to pass by. Seeing the Buddha awake and sitting meditating on his bed of leaves, he approached him and asked:*

'Excuse me, Venerable Lord, but did you sleep well?'

'Yes, Highness, I slept very well. I am certainly one of the best sleepers in the world.'

'But, Venerable One, the winter nights are cold, and this week it froze every morning. The ground is hard, and

CONSCIOUSNESS AS ILLUSION

*the bed of leaves you have on the ground is very thin. Your
robes are thin, too, and the wind that blows is very cold.
Yet you tell me that you slept well, very well?'*

*'Dear Prince, I will ask you a question and you may
reply as you wish. Listen well. Imagine someone living in a
house with a roof that keeps in all the heat, with doors and
windows which shut out the wind. And in this house there
is a couch covered with a thick rug of black wool. Under
the rug are sheets of white linen; at the foot of the couch is
a beautiful antelope skin so the master may step from his
couch without touching the wooden floor. Scarlet cushions
are scattered at the back of the couch, against the wall; a
lamp burns beside it, and four women await the wishes of
the master. What do you think, Highness? Will this man
sleep well or badly?'*

*'Oh, he will surely sleep very well; he must be one
of the best sleepers in the whole world.'*

*'And yet, Highness, do you not think he might have
bad dreams? Doubts born of fear, jealousy, hatred, sorrow,
disillusion – a great number of worries which might stop
him sleeping? Do you not think that he might be afflicted
by illness, by a sickness in his body which might keep him
awake?'*

'Oh of course, Venerable One, of course.'

'You see, Highness, I have cut away the very roots of desire, of hatred, of disillusion, and all that could prevent this man from sleeping well. This, Highness, is the reason I have slept so well. Serene, and free from all attachment, having cut away the chains which could bind me, I have removed all the possibilities of sorrow from within me.'

Later, halting in the village of Sedaka, the Buddha addressed the people who pressed round him:

'Once upon a time there was a tightrope-walker. After he had given his show, he called his assistant and said: "Come here, and climb upon my shoulders."

'"Yes, Master, I am coming."

'He climbed on his master's shoulders. Both went up the ladder to the platform from which the tightrope was strung. Just before he walked along it, the master said:

'"Now, pupil, you look after me well and I will look after you. Like that, looking after each other, we will put on amazing performances. The people will adore us, clap and give us money, and we will come down safe and sound."

'Whereupon the pupil said to the master: "No, no, Master, that will not do at all, that is not the way to do it. You look after yourself, and I will look after myself. If we both look after ourselves, we can put on our show, get down safe and sound and make a good income."

'In fact, neither of those two was completely right, for he who protects himself will protect others. And by protecting others, he will protect himself.

'And how will he protect others by protecting himself? By exercising great vigilance and developing his concentration, so that he is fully aware.

'And how will he protect himself by protecting others? By abstention, non-violence, gentleness and compassion.

'I protect myself – this is the basis of proper awareness. I protect others – this is also the basis of proper awareness. By protecting oneself, one protects others; by protecting others, one protects oneself.'

Kosam~*Kosambi*

This morning we left Varanasi before it was light. We are making for the junction of the Ganges and the Yamuna, scene of a famous festival that takes place every twelve years – the Kumbha-Mela – with its astonishing spectacle of hundreds of thousands of *sadhus* arriving on pilgrimage from all over India. Next, we have to cross the huge bridge and pass through the frightful town of Allahabad. A few more hours' driving and the dirt track peters out in the village of Kosam. Here, all that remains of a fabulously wealthy city in the days of the Buddha are a few wattle-and-daub buildings which peer down over the Yamuna. Various paths lead us to the top of the mounds representing the remains of a fortification more than three-quarters of a mile in circumference. Under a blazing sun, we press on towards a range of gently undulating hills, some of whose slopes shelter cultivated terraces. A handful of excavations, more foundations, but no traces of the structures that were above ground. On a flat space used for winnowing, we find a fragment of one of Asoka's columns. Women pass by with water-pots on their heads – the paths crisscross at this point. But this plain conceals a vast treasure-house, for a whole city is buried beneath its surface. At every step our feet disturb fragments of pottery among the stones, and, where the paths twist and turn, the soil has sunk to reveal remains of what was once the home of thousands.

We are walking on top of a dead city.

A peasant, his scythe over his shoulder, approaches us and guides us through a labyrinth of *tumuli* worn down by the passage of two thousand years. The city died when a plague caused the inhabitants to flee – they never returned, and left the place to the ghosts. This very moment we are walking through Ghositarama Monastery – or rather the skeleton of it brought to light by excavations. In the fifth century BCE, this was a place of great renown, constructed and donated by a rich merchant named Ghosita. The

Buddha stayed here, too. He preached in this flourishing trading city and must have come to know – probably on more than one occasion – the disappointment of seeing his message understood in the letter but not in the spirit.

One day, a monk who had committed a breach of discipline was happy to admit his error, though his brethren did not consider him at fault. Later, however, the monk in question decided he was not guilty, while the others came to believe that he was. The brother's offence was to leave the water in the lavatory pitcher instead of emptying it after he had used it to clean himself.

The accused monk was questioned and admitted it was true. Then a chapter of his brethren was called, and they voted to expel him.

The monk in question was learned and wise, respecting both his religious doctrine and monastic discipline, a man highly accomplished, in fact, in all aspects of his profession. He consulted with his friends and supporters, explaining what had happened and convincing them of his innocence. These went to remonstrate with the group who had expelled their friend and a fierce altercation took place. The matter, however, ended inconclusively.

The monks were now divided into two camps, and the news reached the ears of the Buddha. Noticing how dissension within the community had increased, he sought out the group responsible for the expulsion. He explained to them the folly of their action and the discord it would sow within the community. He then visited the opposing party and rebuked its members as well, with a warning that their actions, too, might provoke a serious rift in the order.

After the Buddha's lecture, the monks who had instigated the expulsion continued with their strict regime inside the monastery, while the opposing faction carried on their rites outside the walls. When the Buddha noticed this, he decided that this was probably the end of the matter.

But it was not to be. With the Kosambi community divided into two hostile camps, their disputes spilled over into the village itself when the two groups went seeking alms – and, in short, whenever they happened to meet. The villagers lost patience with their scandalous behaviour and began to berate and insult them.

A few monks invited the Buddha to intervene and settle things once and for all. He came to the monks' assembly and denounced their conduct. Furthermore, he related the story of King Brahmadatta of Kasi and King

Dighiti of Kosala – as well as what befell Prince Dighavu – with a view to opening their eyes to the dangers of quarrelling and the benefits of moderation.

Recalling the patience and restraint of the two kings, the Buddha encouraged the monks to stop quarrelling, to be equally patient and tolerant, as befitted their occupation. However, a representative of one of the parties demanded that he should withdraw from the dispute and leave them to resolve it on their own. So he left the assembly. 'They are mad,' he declared. 'They have lost their self-control. It is no easy matter to convince them or make them see reason.'

The following day, after he had returned from seeking alms in Kosambi, the Buddha took his meal and addressed the monks on the dangers of strife and discord, as well as the blessings of solitude.

When he had delivered this sermon to the community, he turned his back on the village of Kosambi and set off alone for another village called Balakalonakara. Here, he was received by the Venerable Bhagu. He then went on to the park of Pacinavamsa where there lived the Venerable Amurudha, the Venerable Nandiya and the Venerable Kimbila.

The gate-keeper of the park wanted to turn the

*Buddha away, but the three monks rushed up to receive
him with marks of honour. After having heard them tell
how they lived together on the best possible terms, each
respecting the others, he gave them some advice and left
those parts for the forest of Parileyyaka. Arriving in the forest,
he installed himself at the foot of a handsome sal tree.
Once he was alone, he felt happy and relieved, away from
the Kosambi monks who were always running to him with
their grumbles.*

*Legend has it that a bull elephant, the leader of the
herd, tired of living communally in this forest, resolved to
live alone and no longer wear out his body with the female
elephants when they came out of the water. This elephant
arrived at the spot where the Buddha was sitting and began
waiting on him, bringing him food and drink. So he, too,
discovered a taste for the hermit's life. The Buddha was
loud in his praises of solitude and all its joys.*

Returning to Kosambi two or three months later,
he said:

*'Monks, I will reveal to you the story of the Perfect
Lover of Solitude. Listen, and I will tell you.'*

He went on:

'Let not a man hark back to the past,
Let him not live for the future;
The past stretches far behind him,
And the future is not accessible.
The present, however, he can grasp
As soon as it draws nigh to him.
Impassiveness, detachment.
This is the state the wise man should seek.
Today we must live;
Death may come tomorrow. Who knows?
We can conclude no pact with death,
For his hosts are exceeding strong.
He who with fervour and without respite
Lives his life in isolation:
He it is whom the Wise One has called
The Perfect Lover of Solitude.'

He gave another famous address to his disciples –
seekers and dreamers all – in a wood of *sinsapa* trees:

'Which do you think, monks, are the most

numerous, these few sinsapa *leaves which I hold in my
hand, or the others above us in the* sinsapa *wood?'*

*'These leaves, O Master, that the Blessed One holds
in his hand, are few; much more numerous are those
above our heads in the* sinsapa *wood.'*

*'Likewise, monks, many more things are there which
I have discovered but have not revealed to you, than those
which I have revealed. And why, monks, have I not
revealed them? Because, monks, it brings you no gain,
because it does not advance you in holiness, because it
does not lead you to abandon the things of this world, nor
does it lead to the extinction of all desire, the cessation of
that which is finite, to peace, to wisdom, to
Enlightenment, to nirvana. Therefore such things I have
not revealed to you.'*

A fine example of his perspicacity. He knew all too
well that the experiences of one individual only have a
limited value for another; personal experience is the only
real teacher. And again, why talk of 'another place', of
things which might or could be true, but are liable merely
to be myths? Things which only cause us to dream of
worlds beyond ourselves and which, on the level of

conscious thought, hover about the mind like phantoms, masking the face of reality.

'There are five things which are beyond the power of any Samana, any Brahmin, any god, any Brahma, any being in the universe to prevent. What are these five things? What is doomed to old age must continue to grow old. What is doomed to illness must fall ill. What is doomed to death must die. What is doomed to ruin must fall into ruin. What is doomed to passing away must inevitably pass away. This is what no Samana can prevent, no Brahmin, nor a god, nor Mara, nor Brahma, nor any being in the universe.'

And, at Kosambi, one day when King Pasenadi came on a visit to question the Buddha about his life and teaching, the latter replied:

'Imagine, O King, that a loyal and trustworthy man arrives from the East. Approaching you, he says: "Majesty, I must warn you that I come from the lands of the east; I have seen a great mountain, as tall as the sky, that is heading towards us, crashing down, crushing all living creatures and destroying everything in its path. Heed this

warning, Sire, and do whatever seems fit."

'Then a second man arrives from the west, a third from the north, a fourth from the south. Each of them says: "Majesty, you should know that we come from faraway regions, from all the quarters of the earth, and we have seen a great mountain, as tall as the sky. It is moving and coming towards us, crashing down, and crushing all living creatures in its path. Heed this warning, Sire, and do whatever you think fit."

'And in such a situation, O King, when a terrible danger threatens the destruction of human lives, facing such a catastrophe and considering human life is so precious, what would be your reaction?'

'In such a situation, Master, when the human race is threatened with destruction, and knowing that life is so precious, what else could we do, under such a threat, but practise the dharma, *live quietly, do good works and abide in wisdom?'*

'And yet I tell you, O King, these dangers are ever present. Old age and death will come to you, as they come to everyone. Since they will come inexorably, what will you do?'

'Well, then,' said the king, 'since old age and death

will come to me as they come to everyone, what else can be done save to practise dharma, live in peace, do good works and abide in wisdom?'

One day, the people of the Kalama tribe in Kesaputta came to see the Buddha. After greeting him with hands joined and introducing themselves, they sat down beside him and said:

'Master, why do all the Brahmins and the sannyasins who come to Kesaputta explain and defend their own teachings by criticizing and deriding the doctrines of others? This causes great confusion, and we cannot separate truth from falsehood in their speeches.'

'Yes, it is true: you Kalamas may well be full of doubt because of this. But follow my counsel. Let not your beliefs be founded upon tales handed down, and which people say are the words of a god; nor on the words of an unending series of teachers. Nor let them be founded on gossip nor writings nor speculations and metaphysical theories. Let them not be founded on reason, nor on the authority of the learned, nor on a blind respect for words and acts of religion. Instead, O Kalamas, you must take notice of what leads to sorrow and suffering. For example, if a person is overcome with greed, does he work to his own good, or to his misfortune?'

'To his misfortune, O Blessed One.'

'Indeed, for greed makes a man lose control of his mind and his tongue; he commits evil actions, and sooner or later he will have to repent of them. The same is true of bitterness and delusion, the lot of humanity in its anguish. Then, if you know in your hearts that greed, bitterness and delusion cause evil within you and about you, you must abandon them! Therefore there will be no need to found your beliefs upon the usual things; you Kalamas will live in the proper spirit of religion. For the absence of greed, bitterness and delusion creates neither evil nor suffering. Rather, it leads to a life of righteousness, compassion, equanimity and sympathy for others: an existence which, in every direction, shines forth with abundant and infinite vigour, free from affliction, pure and incorruptible. If you lead such a life, you may be sure of this:

'If there is a life after death, the good fruit of your karma will have won you merit, and you will be uplifted in the world beyond.

'If there is nothing after death, if karma ceases to exist, your righteousness will have saved you from hostility, affliction and sorrow.

'If you have committed many evil actions, but desire to change and no longer create misfortune, then how can you again be subject to evil? And if you do not create bad karma, *how then can you be impure?*

'So, O Kalamas, the man of noble heart, whose being is freed from hostility and affliction, whose being is detached and purified, this man, even in his life on earth, will have attained true knowledge.'

And the Kalamas rejoiced as they heard these words.

'Lord,' they cried, 'You have enlightened us as a lamp lightens the darkness, as it shows the way to those who have eyes to see.'

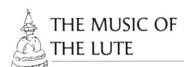

THE MUSIC OF
THE LUTE

Maheth~*Sravasti*

Yet another place where the Buddha stayed each year during the four harsh months of the rains, Sravasti – like most places associated with his name – is merely an archaeological site. Once upon a time there was a vast park; according to legend, Anathapindika, a rich merchant, persuaded its unwilling owner to sell it by covering it with gold pieces.

A monastery was built in the park, one of the most well-appointed of its time, and it sheltered the old bones of the Awakened One for twenty-four seasons. There is not a lot to say, really, except that the foundations are easily seen, revealing the layout of the monastery, the cells and even the house where the Master lived in a room occupying about 75 square feet.

A few miles from this site, in the middle of a forest reached by following an old stony track, there are occasional glimpses of impressive ruins. This is the old city of Sravasti, still largely unexplored. Its ramparts are clearly visible, and the doors give the impression of opening into a forgotten world. Not entirely forgotten, though: herds of skinny cows and goats pass by, driven by young boys who glance suspiciously in our direction. We have been warned not to go out at night and the hotel is guarded by a heavily-armed sentry – there are *dacoits* here, too.

Even more than at Kosam, there is a pervading impression of impermanence. A mood of sadness comes over me as I sit on a mound in the sunset; it is true, everything passes away – people, cities, civilizations. We are mere specks of dust with monstrous egos. So what is mankind's destiny? Yet, as my friend Antonio Taulé – the Catalan painter – is inclined to remark, 'Does every atom agonize over its fate?'

The night is closing in. I climb down the ruins towards the car and leave this place of desolation. On the way back, we pass the monastery where nature broods all alone amid the silence. Here, the Buddha told his patron that there were four legitimate forms of happiness which every layman could enjoy: He could possess sufficient wealth for his needs, if gained by honest means. He could spend this on himself, his friends and relations, as long as he remembered to donate some to the religious fraternity and to help with the building of temples. He could be free from debt. He could lead an upright life, devoid of evil in thought, word and deed.

The first three types of happiness, relating to social and material well-being, are not worth 'the sixteenth part' of the fourth happiness, which reflects a life led in purity of heart. Tirelessly, the Buddha would repeat that existence on a material level, if unenhanced by spiritual effort, was all delusion. This leads us, moreover, to consider his position with regard to political problems.

Profoundly disturbed by the excesses of contemporary rulers and the unhappiness of their subjects, he was the first figure in Indian history known to have rejected the caste system. He allowed pariahs to become monks and disciples, making no distinction between them and the others. Many stories on this subject have been preserved for posterity. One of the most famous stories concerns a woman who earned a pittance by emptying the septic pits and latrines of wealthy houses. She admired the Buddha, but each time she met him she was ashamed of her rags and the nauseating contents of her pitcher, so she crossed to the other side of the street, as she was supposed to do on encountering any Brahmin. One day, however, the Buddha also crossed the street and deliberately stopped her, asking if he could relieve her of her burden. She underwent an immediate transfiguration, so the legend concludes, shedding her rags and losing her hair only to find herself miraculously clothed in a magnificent *kashaya*. The one thing we can be sure of is that the Buddha's actions resulted in her joining the community of nuns, and that she was none the worse for the change.

This compassionate attitude towards other human beings, and outcasts in particular, was quite revolutionary. Only Gandhi, 2,500 years later, would have the courage to tackle this problem in India again.

The Buddha believed, moreover, that any corrupt government would eventually cause its people to degenerate. His actions were not limited to words of peace and preaching non-violence. He was even to visit a battlefield to prevent an armed struggle between Salaya and

Kaliya over the water of a river, and he helped to defuse many a potential conflict in the kingdoms through which he passed. There is a text in the *Jatakas* on the *Ten Duties of a King*, which clearly reveals his opinions on the matter. The duties of a ruler are: to be generous and charitable; to foster high moral values in himself, and therefore to abstain from stealing, killing, exploitation, debauchery and drunkenness; to give priority to the interests of the people; to practise honesty and austerity; to show kindness to one's subjects; to maintain self-control; not to harbour ill-will; to refrain from violence; to exercise patience and tolerance; to be broad-minded and receptive, in harmony with the course of events and the laws of the universe.

The Buddha was evidently recalling the changeless law: 'hatred will never be appeased by hatred, only by compassion'. If only its acceptance were as universal as its truth. King Asoka, in the third century BCE, was to adopt these precepts immediately after his conversion to Buddhism. Once a despot devoted to bloody conquest, he redirected his abilities to the establishment of a brilliant civilization, after taking to heart two of the Buddha's other pronouncements. They are reminiscent of a *hadith* of the prophet Mohammed, used in connection with the concept of Holy War, where a distinction is made between a minor war against others and the major war against oneself:

'A man may conquer in battle, but he who conquers himself is the greatest conqueror of all.
'He who renounces both victory and defeat shall dwell in happiness and tranquillity.'

Asoka is probably the only example in history of a monarch who, at the height of his power, renounced his territorial conquests in order to administer his empire in peace. In one of his famous edicts inscribed on a column of rock, it was written that he

'wished all peoples of the earth peace, self-control and a life of serenity. Conquest through righteousness and piety is the greatest conquest of all.'

He went on to erect columns in all the important places on the Buddha's itinerary.

The Reverend Rahula – a Sri-Lankan Buddhist monk and humanist – puts it like this in his *L'Enseignement du Bouddha*:

Buddhism aims to create a society which renounces the ruinous struggle for power, where tranquillity and peace prevail over victory and defeat; where the persecution of the innocent would be vehemently denounced; where a man who masters himself would earn more respect than one who comes to dominate millions through war or economic conquest. Where hatred would give way to amity and evil to good; where hostility and envy, malevolence and greed would not poison the minds of men; where the driving force of all actions would be compassion; where all living things, including the humblest of creatures, would be treated with justice, consideration and love. Where, in peace, friendship and harmony, in a world where material contentment would be taken for granted, life would be directed towards a nobler and higher goal, the attainment of the ultimate Truth of nirvana.

L'ENSEIGNEMENT DU BOUDDHA (Editions du Seuil, Paris)

This nirvana, dear to all mystics under a variety of names, can be seen as a fusion into the fundamental energy which some call God, a dissolution into the cosmic flux, arrival at the final point, the Omega: the 'Absolute' of Teilhard de Chardin – the ultimate goal of evolution. I myself prefer to consider it as an ascent, one stage of a journey, yet another step on the path to absolute existence.

How much, though, is illusion? We live lives in which reality is what we term the sum of our perceptions; ours is a world where appearances are tangible only for the duration of a glance, a world which the creative power of our 'imago' transforms – for good or otherwise – from moment to moment, a world fashioned as much as experienced by our consciousness. In such a world, even the concept of illusion acquires realities of its own. Again, the experiences of our inner lives declare themselves to be factual. Our understanding of our physical and mental potential is still in its infancy. The Buddha was one of these rare pioneers who yearned to explore the human psyche to its outermost limits.

'Monks, I know nothing which brings more suffering than perception which is neither developed nor cultivated.

'And I know nothing which brings so much happiness as perception which is broadened and cultivated.

'And I know nothing so indocile and intractable and unpromising as perception that is not developed.

'And I know nothing so docile, so tractable and so promising as perception developed every day of our lives.

'I know nothing so conducive to the flowering of evil thoughts and states than unmindfulness. In him who is unmindful arises evil, and what is good vanishes away.

'And I know nothing as powerful to combat these evil states as prudence and vigilance. Whoever has taught himself to lead a prudent and vigilant life and to avoid evil thoughts, he shall be awakened to the higher states of existence.'

One day, King Pasenadi came back to visit the Buddha. After he had prostrated himself, he sat down beside him and said: 'Having retired into a solitary place to meditate, this thought came to me: "Who is the man who loves himself? And who is the man who does not love himself?" I realized then that such as performed evil actions through thought, word or deed, these do not love themselves. Why? Because they do to themselves what a man would do to his enemy. Therefore they cannot love themselves. But those who do good in thought, word or deed, they are such as love themselves, even if they do not know it. They behave to themselves as a friend to a friend.'

The Buddha smiled and replied: 'That is so, O King, that is so.'

The Buddha's enforced retreats during the rainy season allowed him to conduct long sessions with his monks, in which meditations were punctuated by discussion:

'Listen, monks. He who is noted for these four marks of his character should be held to be worthless. What are these four marks?

'A man who is worthless, without prompting, comes forward to denounce others. Then, when he is questioned closely, he speaks of the faults of others, omitting nothing, without the least hesitation, making much play of every detail. Such a man you may consider worthless.

'Furthermore, pressed to reply, the man who is worthless does not care to admit the qualities of others; even less so when he is not pressed. Yet, pressed hard, he will admit what is praiseworthy in others, though grudgingly, and with hesitation. Such a man you may consider worthless.

'As for his own faults, these he keeps hidden. Questioned closely, he begins to admit them, but vaguely and incompletely, forgetting what suits him. Such a man you may consider worthless.

'Furthermore, the worthless man parades his achievements without being asked. Press him with questions, and he will boast even louder.

'A man, monks, who possesses these four traits should be considered as one without merit.

'But, monks, whoever displays the four good qualities, this man should be held to possess a noble mind. What then are these qualities?

'A man of noble mind does not reveal the faults of others, especially when he is asked. However, questioned closely, he alludes to them vaguely and incompletely, omitting some. Such a man, monks, should be considered to possess a noble mind.

'Of his own free will, he speaks good of others. Questioned closely, he relates what is good in others, fully, and in detail. Such a man possesses a noble mind.

'Again, such a man does not boast – especially when not questioned. Pressed to reply, he mentions his good qualities, but vaguely and incompletely. Such a man possesses a noble mind.

'Such a man, who possesses these four qualities, should be considered a man of noble ideas.'

Four Venomous Serpents

One day when the Lord Buddha was staying near Sravasti, he addressed the monks as follows:

'Imagine, monks, four venomous serpents –
extremely dangerous and deadly. Then along comes a man
who wishes to live and not to die, who yearns for happiness
and detests suffering. And the people say to him:
'"My good man, here there are four serpents,
extremely dangerous and venomous; from time to time, it
is necessary to wake them, bathe them, feed them and find
them lodging. But if one or the other of these four serpents
is angered or provoked, then you risk death, or suffering

equally atrocious. Now then, my good man, do what you think best.'

'Think now of this man; terrified by the four venomous serpents, he runs away, and the people say:

"My good man, five murderers are pursuing you. They say that when they catch you, they will kill you. Now do what you think best, my good man."

'Imagine now, monks, that the people say to this man terrified by the four venomous serpents and the five murderers:

'"My good man, a sixth, a fearsome bandit, brandishing a sabre, is pursuing you. He says that when he catches you, he will chop off your head. Now then, my good man, do what you think best."

'And this man, terrified by the four venomous serpents, the five murderers and the fearsome bandit, runs away. He sees a deserted village; each house he enters is empty. Then some passers-by say to him:

'"My good man, the bandits who attack villages will attack this deserted village. Now then, do what you think best."

'This man, terrified by the venomous serpents, the five murderers, the fearsome bandit and the men attacking

the village, runs away. He espies a great stretch of water. The near bank is exposed to danger, and therefore to be avoided. The other bank is far off, but safe and secure. Yet there is no boat or bridge by which he can reach this other bank.

'Then an idea comes to him. "Here is a great stretch of water, but there is neither boat nor bridge. Why do I not collect up grass, pieces of wood, branches and leaves, and make a raft with which to reach the other bank, using my hands and feet as oars?"

'The Brahmin crossed the water, and now stands on dry land.'

'Monks, this is a parable, and here is its meaning:

'The four venomous and dangerous serpents are the four elemental forces of nature: earth, fire, water, air.

'The five murderers are the five aggregates of human existence: body, sensation, perception, mental activity and consciousness.

'The sixth, the fearsome bandit brandishing his sabre, represents pleasure and attachment.

'The deserted village stands for the six fundamental senses; if a wise and intelligent man examines the eye, the ear, the mind, each appears empty and without substance.

'The men attacking the village represent the six fundamental senses, for the eye is tormented by visible objects which attract or repel it, the ear and the mind are besieged by things which attract or repel them, things connected with the mind.

'The broad stretch of water represents the four fluxes: continual cravings, the future, ideas and ignorance.

'The bank exposed to danger and therefore to be avoided represents the world of delusion, of many delusions.

'The other bank, free from danger, represents nirvana.

'The raft is the Noble Eightfold Path, that is to say: perfect view, perfect resolve, perfect speech, perfect conduct, perfect livelihood, perfect effort, perfect mindfulness, perfect concentration.

'The hands and feet which turn themselves into oars: they are sustained effort.

'As for the Brahmin who crossed the river, he is the man who has achieved perfection.'

The Buddha's teaching became more and more profound as the years passed, though still based on simple, practical things: meditation and the psychology of action. What, we ask, are the Three Roots of Action?

'Suppose, monks, wandering ascetics from other sects question you and say: "There exist three states – that of desire, that of hatred and that of delusion or error. What are the distinctions to be made between these three states; what are their meanings and their differences?" Questioned thus, what will you answer?'

'"Lord, all teaching has its roots in your words. If you will be pleased to guide us on this subject and make it clear, we, your monks, will be able to understand, and later we will be able to answer."

'Then listen carefully. If you are questioned thus, you may reply: "Desire is the least reprehensible state, but the hardest to avoid. Hatred is more reprehensible, but easier to suppress. Error or delusion is exceedingly reprehensible and difficult to root out from our actions."

'And now, O my friends, what is the reason for the appearance and increase of desire? An object of beauty, perhaps. Whoever accords unjustified importance to an object of beauty will suffer the appearance and increase of desire.

'And O my friends, what is the root of the appearance and increase of hatred? Something which repels us will, if we are not careful, give rise to hatred.

'And, O my friends, whence comes error, whence the appearance and increase of delusion in our lives? Unmindfulness is the cause of the appearance and increase of error in our daily lives.

'And now, O my friends, whence arises the non-appearance of desire, and its disappearance? "Impurity" might be the answer. Indeed, whoever sees what is repugnant and impure and repulsive in a body or an object, this person does not experience the arousal of desire, nor its disappearance.

'And, O my friends, what is the cause of the non-appearance and the disappearance of hatred? "The liberation of the heart: the awakening of a state of love and compassion", might be the answer. If a person devotes his attention to creating within him feelings of compassion, kindness and love, he discovers that hatred has departed from him.

'And finally, O my friends, what shall be the reason for the non-appearance of error? The answer lies in mindfulness and wisdom. If a person is mindful and *develops wisdom in his conscious thoughts, he finds that the state in which errors arise has departed from him, he deludes himself no longer, and, in his daily life, transgresses less.'*

Existence

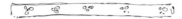

*One day, the Venerable Ananda came to see the Buddha
and asked him a question:*

*'We have been discussing existence. Tell me, Lord,
what is the cause of existence?'*

'Ananda, if there were no karma *– no action –
arising in the lower sphere of the five senses, would it be
possible for sensation to exist?'*

'By no means.'

'Then, Ananda, karma *and its action are like a field;
consciousness is the seed, and insatiable desire is the
moisture necessary for its germination. Fettered by
ignorance and enchained by desire, consciousness is*

imprisoned within this lower sphere of the five senses.

'And, Ananda, if karma did not arise in the sphere of the five senses, would these latter exist?'

'Assuredly not, Lord.'

'Then, Ananda, the action of karma, the action of our own actions, this is the field; consciousness of this is the seed, and insatiable desire is the moisture which allows sensation to germinate.

'Thus, fettered by ignorance and enslaved by the force of desire, consciousness is imprisoned within this intermediate sphere.

'Finally, Ananda, if there were no karma arising in an immaterial sphere, how could anything exist that was not matter? This is why, Ananda, action is the field, consciousness the seed, and desire the moisture.

'Fettered by ignorance and enslaved by desire, consciousness infiltrates itself into this upper sphere of immaterial things. This, Ananda, is the origin of future, incarnation and birth.

'This is the origin of existence.'

'There are, monks, three sorts of speculations which, if they are taken to their conclusion, lead to a doctrine based on inaction and the negation of the law of cause and

effect, the negation of interdependence, the negation of
karma.

'Certain monks and ascetics defend one of these
three doctrines. For example, some of them say that
whatever a person's experiences, happiness, sorrow or
neutral state of mind, they arise from actions accomplished
during a previous life.

'Others teach that the pleasures, pains and neutral
states experienced by man are solely the result of divine
creation.

'Finally, others proclaim that pleasure, pain and
indifference are not subject to cause and effect, and have no
basis in reality.

'But, having debated with these ascetics and
Brahmins, I say to them: if in truth our experiences have
their root in previous lives, or in divine creation, or have no
reality of their own, what of those who kill, steal and cheat;
what of those who dwell in error, greed, debauchery, lies,
baseness and evil-doing? Are their actions the result of
previous lives or of divine creation?

'What is more, if a person believes that human
actions are decided by previous lives or divine creation, or
that pleasure, pain and indifference are not real, he will

203

always lack energy, motives, effort and determination; he will not accomplish this, he will not abandon that. He is ignorant about how to live his life; how then can he guide others?

'These three doctrines, monks, if they become accepted, lead only to inaction and amorality. These ideas may be said to be divisive.

'Now, monks, hear what I will tell you; hear what cannot be so refuted, hear the teaching of the dharma ... *There exist six elements, six spheres of sensory perception, eighteen mental approaches and Four Noble Truths.*

'The six elements are: earth, air, fire, water, space, consciousness.

'The six spheres of sensory perception are: the ear, the eye, the nose, the tongue, the body, and the mind.

'The eighteen mental approaches are as follows: when we see with the eye the visual image of an object, this approach can give rise to pleasure, sadness, or indifference. Likewise, to hear a sound with the ears, to smell a smell with the nose, to taste a taste with the tongue, to feel with the body, to experience a thought with the mind – each of these approaches can bring pleasure, sadness or indifference. All in all, this makes

eighteen mental approaches.

'What now are the Four Noble Truths of the dharma that I teach? As a result of the six elements, life manifests itself in the womb of woman. As a result of body and consciousness arise the six senses, the servants of sensation and perception. And for human beings so conceived, who have the power to exist, to feel, and to react consciously, I declare these Four Truths:

'Suffering exists. There is an origin of suffering. There is a cessation of suffering.

'But, monks, what is the Noble Truth of Suffering? Birth is suffering, old age is suffering, sickness, death, sorrow, pain, remorse, anguish and despair: all are suffering. Association with those whom we hate – that is suffering. Separation from those whom we love – that is suffering. Not to obtain what we desire – that is suffering. In fact, the five aggregates of attachment are all suffering.

'And what, O my bothers, is the Noble Truth of the Origin of Suffering?

'As a result of ignorance, karma arises. As a result of karma, consciousness arises. The result of consciousness is body-and-mind. Body-and-mind disposes of six senses, which give rise to six impressions, that is, all forms of

THE MUSIC OF THE LUTE

sensation. As a result of sensation desire arises, which, in turn, leads to attachment. Attachment gives rise to incarnations, that is, rebirths. And birth itself sets us on the road to suffering, ageing, sorrow, weariness and death. This is the origin of what we call suffering.

'And what, monks, is the Noble Truth of the Cessation of Suffering?

'When ignorance is dissipated and extinguished, karma *disappears. Extinguished, too, is all that leads to suffering. But then, monks, how may we arrive at the Noble and True Way which leads to this goal? By the Noble Eightfold Path, which is: perfect view, perfect resolve, perfect speech, perfect conduct, perfect livelihood, perfect effort, perfect mindfulness, perfect concentration.*

'Such is the Way, which no man may disavow, neither ascetic nor Brahmin, nor any person of intelligence.'

But one question remains. How would the Buddha perceive the notion of God and His existence?

In all probability like this:

'Vasettha, is there a single one of the Brahmins

learned in the three Vedas who has met Brahma face
to face?

'No, Gautama, assuredly not.'

'Vasettha, has there existed a single one of their
pupils, or of their teachers up to the seventh generation,
who has met Brahma face to face?'

'Not to my knowledge, Gautama.'

'Then why do all the Brahmins continually chant
these verses of the ancient rishis: "We know God, we have
seen Him where He is and as He is; we know who is
Brahma"? In fact, Vasettha, what they say is this: "What
we have neither seen nor felt, this union which we have not
experienced, such is the direct way which leads to Brahma,
such is the way of salvation." It seems to me, therefore,
that the Brahmins are foolish. They seem to me like blind
men roped together, or like the man who built steps to a
house which did not exist. These Brahmins seem to me like
a busy man who, wishing to cross a river in flood, shouts
to the opposite bank: "O bank, come over to this side and
fetch me!" In the same way, the Brahmins chant over and
over the names of their gods: "O Indra, O Soma, O
Brahma, O Yama, hear our cry!" But the gods remain
silent, just as the opposite bank will not come to fetch the

foolish and stupid man who calls it. The behaviour of these Brahmins lacks sense; the behaviour of these Brahmins lacks wisdom.'

Evolution

Teilhard de Chardin had a vision of man as the pivot and the arrowhead of evolution. But does Buddhism share this view? The Buddha considered it was necessary to escape the ceaseless cycle of births and deaths; to achieve this, humanity must awake to the ultimate reality of the universe and acquire the clarity of vision which results from Enlightenment. Such a viewpoint, very Brahminic and constantly recurring in the *Vedas*, brings into play the concept of reincarnation. In actual fact, the Buddha never mentioned this specifically except when relating his Awakening under the Bodhi Tree; from then on, he refused outright to discuss what happened after death, focusing his teaching on the practicalities of daily life and the perfecting of the mind. Several of the *sutras* express his determination on this point:

'What is universe? Nothing but the eye and visible objects, the ear and sounds, the nose and odours, the tongue and tastes, the body and tangible objects, consciousness and the phenomena of consciousness. That is what people call universe.'

A parable asks us to imagine a king who had never before heard the sound of the lute (*vina*). On hearing it for the first time, he exclaims:

'Whence comes this sound: so fascinating, captivating and wondrous?' 'It is the sound of a lute, Sire.' 'Bring it to me.' But once his courtiers have brought it to him, the king says: 'I do not want this thing; I only want the sound.' The courtiers reply: 'What is called a lute is composed of many parts. There is the neck, the sound box, the plectrum and the strings: when everything is put together properly and a man plays it with his fingers, it makes the sound you desire.' But the king, disappointed

and caring only for the sound, smashes the lute to pieces,
burns the pieces, and throws the ashes to the winds,
exclaiming that it is all a trick.

Similarly, a human being is the sum of parts: body, sensations, perceptions, mental activity, consciousness. For the Buddha, investigating these components, under-standing their mechanisms and learning to control them was the only important thing. In his message, the respect for life – this 'unique wave-form', this 'lonely impulse', which, in Teilhard's terminology, has managed to propagate itself on Earth – is found side by side with a determination to extinguish desire. The combination appears contradictory. Yet, when we realize that the Buddha was attacking the very root of delusion, the paradox vanishes. Humanity dreams up the world, allows itself to be ensnared by its phantasms, cutting itself off from life and its natural evolutionary impulse. Now to accomplish its aims, the evolutionary process must ceaselessly undergo mutations, heading all the while in an upward direction. To quote Teilhard:

'In man, considered as a zoological species, various
behaviour patterns are perpetuated: sexual attraction, in

accordance with the laws of reproduction; the will to live, with its inseparable instinct for competition; the need for food and the impulse to find and eat it; curiosity to make discoveries, including the pleasure accompanying investigation; the desire to join with others and live in societies ... Each of these instincts is like a fibre running through our bodies, starting from somewhere before us and ending up somewhere after us; the consequence is that each of these fibres contains in epitome the whole of evolutionary history – as true a history as any. Within them is stored the evolution of love, of war, discovery, society ... But in addition, each one, precisely because it is still undergoing evolution, experiences a metamorphosis under the effect of thought and reflection. After which it sets off again into the future, enriched with new possibilities, new colours, a new fertility. In one sense, it is the same; in another, something completely different. Think of a shape, and how it alters with a change in volume or dimensions ... Or again, discontinuity imposed upon continuity. Mutation upon evolution.

In the course of this subtlest of transmutations, in this harmonious process of reshaping which transfigures the whole network – externally and internally – of vital

antecedents, it is surely impossible not to discover an
invaluable confirmation of what intuition has already led
us to believe. When an object begins to develop in only one
part of itself, it loses its symmetry and becomes misshapen.
To retain its symmetry and its beauty, it must develop in all
parts simultaneously, following some of its principal axes.
When the learning process interacts with a species, this
does not erase the existing patterns, only modifies or
rearranges them. There is no question of the fortuitous
outgrowth of a parasitic energy. Man only progresses by
slowly modifying, from age to age, the essence and totality
of the universe within him.'

LE PHÉNOMÈNE HUMAIN (Editions du Seuil, Paris).

Today, at the start of a new millennium, humanity
does appear to have evolved inordinately in a single respect
– in its ability to deploy discriminatory thought, boastful of
its omnipotence and its discoveries. Yet our species has
never before been so threatened by itself. And the Buddha's
message, like that of Christ, is eternal. Both lived and uttered
their wisdom in their own times, but the essence of their
arguments retains its validity. Both looked to the world to
come, a world beyond man, yet primarily existing within

him. It is not a question of refuting the powers of thought and scientific knowledge; nor is there any question of regressing to some mythical golden age, or severing ourselves from reality. Rather, we need to infiltrate reality by a process resembling osmosis, in full awareness of its delusions, its evolutionary errors and the inevitable and necessary decomposition of every system, and, ultimately, by an acceptance of death, 'that essential cog in the mechanism and rise of life' (Teilhard de Chardin). And, in this century which has left its vivid and frenetic brush-strokes on the unfolding canvas of history, the words of the Buddha still ring true as he speaks of 'gardens lying fallow, which we need to cultivate within us':

'Monks, two things contribute to knowledge: the peacefulness of silence, and inner contemplation.

'If we develop inner peace and silence, what is the result? The result is that consciousness develops, too. And what do we gain from the development of consciousness? Desires and cravings are seen for what they are, and we learn to abandon them.

'If we develop inner peace and silence, what is the result? The result is that wisdom develops, too. And what

do we gain from the development of wisdom? We learn to
abandon all forms of ignorance, to cut it off at its roots.

'Consciousness beset by desires is in fetters. Wisdom
troubled by ignorance is in chains. Thus we may rid
ourselves of desires by emancipating our minds; we may rid
ourselves of ignorance by setting wisdom free.'

THE ENDING
OF DAYS

Kasia~*Kusinagara*

Week has followed week, and we have seen so many places: the Buddha was a tireless traveller outside the monsoon season, never resting his feet for long. We have covered around 2,000 miles in the course of our single journey; he was forever coming and going ... until he reached Kusinagara. Now aged over eighty, he was returning to the land of his childhood, an old lion overcome with weariness. But here he finally fell victim to dysentery and fever and died.

The spot where his body was burned is marked by two *stupas*. Everywhere there is an atmosphere of sadness which brings a lump to the throat. Since the Buddha's death, no plants that have been introduced here will grow. There are no flowers with a scent. Nature appears to be in eternal mourning.

This does not prevent the temple guard from trying to appropriate the ten rupees I have earmarked for the donation box and the maintenance of the place. For him, it represents two days' wages. In this temple, there is a magnificent fifth-century effigy of the Buddha, showing him recumbent, in the state of *parinirvana*.

A stone block in a nearby village commemorates the Buddha's last meal in the house of a poor smith. In this miserable village we meet several women who have just given birth to their babies and are rubbing them gently with oil. Life and death are never far apart.

At Beluva, near Vesali, the Buddha spent his last monsoon in total retreat. He was already ill. He gave a sermon on his imminent death after reflecting:

'It is not fitting that I should enter nirvana without speaking to the community of disciples. I intend, by the force of my will, to overcome this illness and hold back my death.'

And the Blessed One, by the force of his will,

overcame his illness and held back death. The illness left
him. As soon as he felt strong enough, he left the house
and sat in its shade on the seat that had been prepared for
him. And the Venerable Ananda came to the Blessed One.
Sitting beside him, he said:

'I see that the Blessed One is well; I see that the
Blessed One is better. My strength had abandoned me,
Lord; my thoughts whirled around, my mind could not
imagine that the Blessed One was truly ill. None the less
this idea reassured me: "The Blessed One will not enter
nirvana before he has made known his will concerning the
community of disciples."'

And the Blessed One replied:

'What does the community of disciples further
require of me, O Ananda? I have made known the doctrine,
O Ananda, I have made no distinction between what is
within and what is without. "He who thinks, O Ananda: I
wish to rule over the community of disciples", or "Let the
community of disciples be subject to me", that person may
make known his intentions concerning the community. But
the Perfect One, O Ananda, does not have this thought: "I
wish to rule over the community of disciples", or "Let the
community of disciples be subject to me". Why, O Ananda,

should the Perfect One go forth and make known his
intentions concerning the community? I am frail now, O
Ananda, I am old, I am an old man with white hair; I have
reached the end of my journey, I am full of years. I am
eighty now, Ananda ...

'Be unto yourselves your own lantern, O Ananda,
and your own refuge. Seek no other refuge but yourselves.
Let the Truth be your lantern and your refuge; seek no
other refuge but this ... From the hour, O Ananda, when
I depart, such as shall be a lantern and a refuge unto
themselves and shall seek no other refuge; such as shall
make of the Truth their lantern and their refuge and shall
seek no other refuge, these shall henceforth, O Ananda,
be my true disciples, and shall walk in the path of
righteousness.'

And, three months later, arriving at Kusinagara, he
exhorted the disciples grouped around him not to lament
in vain. His final words were:

'In truth I say to you, all that is created shall pass
away. Continue the struggle on earth. Never falter.'

And so the Lion of Enlightenment passed the final threshold, having pushed back the frontiers of consciousness to encompass the infinite:

'I tell you this. In this fathom-long body with all its teeming thoughts, there is the whole world, and the origin of the world, and its cessation ...'

And the countless steps of the Way.

APPENDICES

Key Dates in the History of Buddhism

c. 555 BCE   Birth of the Buddha at Lumbini.

c. 530 BCE   Aged about twenty-five, the Buddha leaves his family and tribe. In Greece, the birth of Aeschylus.

c. 520 BCE   First sermons in the Deer Park near Varanasi. After the Buddha's Enlightenment, he begins the 'Turning of the Wheel'. In China, death of Lao Tzu, founder of Taoism.

486 BCE   First Buddhist Council, assembling most of the disciples at Rajagrha (Rajgir) under the leadership of Mahakashyapa.

c. 475 BCE   Death, aged eighty, at Kusinagara (Kasia). The Buddha's ashes are scarcely cold before legend replaces history. Confucius dies in China; in Greece, the birth of Socrates and Empedocles.

383 BCE   Second Council at Vesali.

325 BCE	Alexander the Great reaches India. Beginnings of Greco-Buddhist art.
322 BCE	Death of Aristotle.
c. 250 BCE	Introduction of Buddhism to Ceylon (Sri-Lanka).
247 BCE	In the reign of Asoka, Third Council at Pataliputra (Patna): schism between the Theravada (or Hinayana – 'Small Vehicle' – the Buddhism of the south) and Mahayana ('Great Vehicle' – the form of Buddhism flourishing in the north, forerunner of Ch'an in China and later of Zen in Japan).
c. 240 BCE	Conversion of the Indian emperor Asoka, whose conquests favour the spread of Buddhism in India; the present-day evidence is found on his stone pillars. In China, construction of the Great Wall.
236 BCE	Death of Asoka and decline of his empire.
80 BCE	Spread of the great Mahayana *sutra*, *The Lotus of the True Law*.
1st century CE	Expansion of Buddhism in Nepal and China.
2nd century CE	Nagarjuna, on the basis of the Buddha's teaching, lays down the main foundations of the Madhymika school of Buddhism.

3rd century CE	Expansion of Buddhism into Vietnam and Cambodia.
4th century CE	Further expansion into northern China and Korea.
5th century CE	Indian journey in the footsteps of the Buddha made by the philosopher, Fa'shien. Foundation of the Buddhist University at Nalanda in India. Spread of the Theravada in Burma and Sumatra.
6th century CE	Bodhidharma founds Chinese Buddhism – characterized by the practice of intensive meditation and 'bare-handed' martial arts for self-defence. Foundation of the famous monastery at Shao-lin in China, the cradle of these arts. Spread of Buddhism in Japan, where it is given favoured status by the regent, Shotoku Taishi. Becomes state religion in 610.
7th century CE	First Buddhist temples in Tibet. Birth of Islam with the appearance of the Koran in 630.
8th century CE	Nara period in Japan (710–94) and first large Tibetan monastery (749) at Padmasambhava. Dengyo Daishi (767–822) founds Tendai, esoteric branch of Japanese Buddhism.
9th century CE	Cult of the Amida Buddha in Japan.

10th century CE   In Tibet, the shamanic religion, Bon, comes into conflict with Buddhist monasticism, resulting in persecutions. Advance of Islam in Central Asia.

13th century CE   Destruction of the university at Nalanda by Islamic warriors. Introduction of Ch'an (early type of Zen) to Japan by Dogen Zenji (1200–53), founder of the Soto school, and by Eisai Zenji (1141–1215). The latter perpetuates the work of Lin-chi I-shuan, a Chinese master of the ninth century, and founds Rinzai Zen. In 1282, Nichiren, also in Japan, develops a new Buddhist sect. During this century, the emperor Kublai Khan (1270–94) encourages the development of Buddhism in China; similarly, in Japan, the Shogun favours Zen.

14th century CE   Development of Buddhism in Laos and Siam.

15th century CE   Tsongkhapa, Tibetan Buddhist reformer, founds the sect known as Gelugpas (Yellow Bonnets).

16th century CE   Foundation of the Kum Bum monastery in Tibet.

17th century CE   Construction of the Potala at Lhasa and enthronement of the fifth Dalai Lama (1642–43).

18th century CE   In France, Aquetil Duperron founds a new
                     university course – Oriental Studies.
                     Translates several sacred texts into French,
                     including the Hindu *Upanishads*.

19th century CE   Schopenhauer, the German philosopher,
                     introduces Buddhist teaching to Europe. In
                     the United States, with Emerson and Walt
                     Whitman, oriental thought becomes the
                     symbol of the struggle against a mechanistic
                     interpretation of the mind and in favour of
                     more profound inner development.

20th century CE   René Guenon, Alexandra David-Neel, Jean
                     Herbert, Hermann Hess, D.T. Suzuki, and
                     Aldous Huxley, followed by Alan Watts and
                     the poets of the Beat Generation, disseminate
                     Buddhist texts and theories in the West.

1950s   Chinese invasion of Tibet; flight of fifteenth
                     Dalai Lama.

1960s onwards   Taisen Deshimaru and D.T. Suzuki begin to
                     teach *zazen*, a seated form of Zen meditation.
                     Leading Tibetan *lamas* introduce Buddhism
                     to Europe and the USA. Noticeable increase
                     in the practice of Zen and the number of
                     lama monasteries.

October 1979   Conference of World Buddhist Fellowship in Japan, at Tokyo and Kyoto. Major conclusion: if Buddhism is to grow and flourish, its roots must be kept vigorous. It is therefore essential that meditation is practised properly and rigorously, following the example of the Buddha.

2000 CE   At the start of the 21st century, it is estimated that there are four million practising Buddhists living in the West. The worldwide Buddhist population is thought to be around 350 million.

Brief Glossary

Ananda   A chief disciple and cousin of the Buddha.

arhat   Saint; ascetic in search of his own
                  deliverance. The ideal figure of Theravada; in
                  Mahayana, the equivalent is *bodhisattva*.

Bimbisara   King of Magadha at the time of the Buddha.
                  An early convert to Buddhism, he donated
                  the Bamboo Park for the use of the first
                  sangha.

Brahma   The supreme god of Hinduism.

Brahmin   Hindu belonging to the highest caste (priests).

bodhi   The highest state of mind, reflecting the
                  spirit. Absolute knowledge – Awakening.

Bodhidharma   Twenty-eighth Patriarch after the Buddha and
                  first Patriarch of Ch'an. Born in Ceylon (Sri
                  Lanka) in the fifth century, he appears to
                  have arrived in southern China in 520, aged
                  over sixty. For nine years he practised *zazen*
                  sitting facing a wall in a cave in northern

China. Passed on the succession to Hui-k'o, his first Chinese disciple. Died at very advanced age.

bodhisattva   A person who has reached Enlightenment and is ready to become a Buddha. However, in order to guide humanity to deliverance, he remains in the world of suffering; his activities, devoid of all attachment, are pure compassion. In Zen, this title is given to lay disciples who have taken the Four Vows without retiring from the world; their undertaking is less solemn than that of monks.

dharma   From the Sanskrit root *dhri* meaning to hold, carry, or fix. The order of things, the cosmic system, the law of the Buddha, the absolute Truth. Used in the plural, the word signifies phenomena subject to these – both thoughts and objects.

Dogen   Zen monk (1200–53) who introduced *zazen* to Japan. Following his initiation in China, Dogen travelled to Japan where he founded the Soto school and the temple of Daibutsuji, now known as Eihei-ji (Monastery of Eternal Peace) and still the principal Soto temple. Author of numerous treatises.

Eckhart, Meister German Christian mystic (c.1260–1327).

ghat In India, a passage (often steps) leading to water; used for bathing or ritual cleansing.

hara The central point of the body, situated three finger-breadths below the navel. In *zazen*, the point where exhalation of the breath is concentrated.

Heidegger, Martin
German existentialist philospher (1889-1976).

Jainism Ancient Indian religion, still flourishing today, which stresses the importance of non-injury (*ahimsa*). The greatest of the Jain teachers was Mahavira.

Jatakas Stories of the Buddha's previous lives.

karma Acts, actions or deeds as producers of consequences and psychic residues – positive, negative or neutral. The continuous process of cause and effect. The 'fall-out' which chains us to the cycle of rebirth – and death. See *samsara*.

kashaya The robe worn by the Buddha, made of scraps of old material. A sort of toga which monks wear draped around their bodies in such a way as to leave the right arm free.

Large and rectangular, it is dyed a neutral
colour, and made of several pieces sewn
together in a way symbolising the layout
of rice fields. In theory, a Zen monk sews his
own *kashaya*. It is ceremonially presented to
him by the master at his ordination.

kinhin   In Zen, a walking exercise in which the steps
coincide with the breathing. Forming part of
zazen, it is conducted in the *dojo*, between
two periods of seated meditation. Supposed
to recall the pacing of the Buddha after his
Enlightenment under the Bodhi Tree – when
he decided to pass on his experiences.

Kshatriya Hindu belonging to the second caste (princes,
nobles and warriors). The first was reserved
for Brahmins. The Buddha was a Kshatriya.

lama   Tibetan Buddhist monk.

Lotus Sutra *Saddharmapundarika-sutra: Sutra of the
White Lotus of the True Law*. Chinese: *Miao
fa Xian hua jing.* Japanese: *Myoho-renge-kyo.
Adoration of the Lotus of Perfect Truth.* One
of the seminal texts of Mahayana Buddhism,
dating probably from the first century.

Mahayana   The 'Great Vehicle' or northern Buddhism
(Tibet, Mongolia, China, Korea, Japan),

including Zen. It promulgates the ideal figure of the *bodhisattva*, as opposed to the *arhat* in Theravada.

Mahakashyapa Indian ascetic. The Buddha admitted him on the spot to the band of disciples, bidding him share his seat as a mark of honour. Mahakashyapa succeeded to the leadership of the *sangha* (assembly of disciples) after the Master's death.

Mahavira Spiritual leader of the Jains at the time of the Buddha (he lived 599–527/510 BCE). Seen today as the greatest of Jainism's teachers.

Mara The Spirit of Evil and the embodiment of death.

Maya Sanskrit for 'delusion' or 'illusion' and also the name given to the Buddha's mother.

Middle Way General term for the path to Enlightenment as practised and taught by the Buddha; a practice which avoids the extremes of ascetiscism and self-gratification.

mudra Mystical gesture of the hands which carries a symbolic meaning.

Nagarjuna Indian philosopher of the second century, fourteenth patriarch after the Buddha, one of the founders of Mahayana Buddhism.

Namuci	'The Tempter' – another name for Mara.
nirvana	The cessation of suffering; the end of attachments and passions; the end of existence conditioned by cause and effect and subsequent return to the absolute Original.
paramita	The Six Perfections or fundamental virtues of Buddhism, including *prajna*, fully attainable only by a *bodhisattva*, and, of course, a Buddha.
parinirvana	Complete extinction, absolute deliverance; state attained by the Buddha after his death.
prajna	Intuitive knowledge, supreme wisdom.
pranayama	Control of the breathing. Known as *prana* in Sanskrit, breathing is considered to be the agent of cosmic energy.
Rinzai	One of the two principal remaining schools of Zen. Originated with Lin-chi (Japanese Rinzai) – a great master of Chinese Ch'an in the Tang dynasty – who died in 867 CE. Rinzai was introduced into Japan by Eisai Myoan (1141–1215).
sadhu	Holy person who has renounced the world in order to search for God.

samadhi | Eighth and last degree of yoga: a state of profound meditation, perfect single-pointed concentration, free from all attachment and producing complete unification in the practitioner.

samsara | Birth-and-death; the universal law of transmigration, escapable only by the passage into nirvana.

sangha | In Buddhism, the community of disciples or monks.

sannyasin | In Hinduism, a person in the fourth and final stage of life, who renounces worldly and family ties in order to become a beggar.

Sariputra | One of the first and most senior disciples of the Buddha; he died before his Master.

skandha | Aggregate or group of phenomena. According to Buddhism, we are composed of five aggregates: *rupa* or form; *vedana* or sensation; *samjna* or perception; *samskara* or mental formations; *vijnana* or awareness.

Soto | One of the two great present-day schools of Zen, the largest in Japan in terms of the number of temples and followers. Founded in the thirteenth century, it is named after two

Chinese Masters: Tung-shan Liang-chieh
(Japanese: Tozan Ryokai) and his disciple
Ts'ao-shan Pen-chi. (In Chinese, the school
was called Ts'ao-tung after the first character
of each founder's name; this becomes 'Soto'
in Japanese.)

stupa   Domed monument with spire which
symbolizes Buddhahood. Originally, a royal
funeral mound.

sutra   Literally 'thread', particularly that used to
string a necklace. A speech or sermon
allegedly uttered by the Buddha or one of
his immediate disciples.

Tathagata   The 'Thus come' or 'Thus-perfected One'.
A Buddha.

Teilhard de Chardin, Pierre
French Jesuit theologian and palaeontologist
(1881-1955). He travelled widely in Asia
during the 1920s and 1930s. His theory of
universal evolution, argued in *Le Phénomène
Humain* and *Le Milieu Divin*, states that
humanity is evolving, through increasingly
close-linked social relationships and
consciousness, towards a totally integrated
Absolute, or Omega.

Theravada　　The 'School of the Ancients', referring to southern Buddhism (Sri-Lanka, Burma, Thailand, Vietnam). Also called Hinayana, the 'Small Vehicle' by the followers of Mahayana, the 'Great Vehicle'; 'small' because Theravada emphasizes personal deliverance, while the Mahayana aims at universal liberation.

Vedas　　Hindu sacred texts dating back 4,000 years.

zazen　　Type of Zen practising seated meditation. Advocated by the Buddha as essential for those seeking the Noble Eightfold Path leading to the cessation of suffering through: perfect view, perfect resolve, perfect speech, perfect conduct, perfect livelihood, perfect effort, perfect mindfulness, perfect concentration.

The practitioner must concentrate on the correct posture – full of dignity – and on deep breathing, exhaling right down to the *hara*. He or she should regard thoughts as a window into the mind; they are projected continuously on to our inner 'screen', like a film of our hopes, fears and dreams, and serve as a unique form of self-analysis.

The practitioner who observes these rules may attain a state where energy, mental equilibrium and detachment transform him or her into a new person.

Each being contains the Buddha-nature; it is up to that being to discover it.